OBSERVATIONS FROM THE 2.0 CAFÉ

"If you plan on either having employees, or being one in the 'Epoch of Uncertainty' then this book is for you. Employees will be every firm's most valuable *investor*. It's now up to the company to make, as Jensen puts it, the new work environment into an 'elegant tool'."

Watts Wacker, FirstMatter LLC, coauthor,
The 500-Year Delta and *The Visionary's Handbook*

"Bill Jensen has drawn the roadmap for effective leadership in the twenty-first century. Five years from now, we will have failed as leaders if we have not addressed these issues! I am convinced that extreme leadership will be critical in a rapidly changing world."

Michael A. Volkema, Chairman, President and CEO, Herman Miller, Inc.

"The kinds of employees described in *Work 2.0* are not the thin edge of the wedge. Nearly a third of Americans in the labor force already identify themselves as 'emergent workers': having skills in high demand, comfortable with leading-edge technology, and ready to work in unconventional situations. Jensen points the way to understanding this oncoming wave of workers, and refashioning their organizations to unleash both productivity and passion."

Hank McKinnell, Chairman and CEO, Pfizer, Inc.

"Bill Jensen is the business Copernicus of his age. He's established that everything revolves around getting and keeping great people. This law holds in good times and bad. All objections are simply Ptolomeic!"

Thomas H. Davenport, Director, Accenture Institute for Strategic Change, and Distinguished Scholar, Babson College

"*Work 2.0* does the best job yet of accurately defining the real enemy in the war for talent — ourselves and the cultures we have created. Bill's direct, compelling writing style answers the question of how we can live every day with courage, compassion, and the depth of character required to succeed as 'extreme leaders' in this next evolution of work and people."

John Harvey, Senior Vice President, Global Talent, American Express

"Bill Jensen's new work provides us with a powerful message of hope. People do matter, perhaps now more than ever. *Work 2.0* correctly reveals why life, and ideas, and the marketplace are so interdependent. Innovation and compassion meet brilliantly in this very timely work."

Bill Strickland, Executive Director, Manchester Craftsmen's Guild

"Jensen's book is an in-your-face elegant treatise on the holy trinity of technology, traffic, and trust. He delivers the hard facts of primordial and ancient accountabilities (or what revisionist historians label as 'new economy metrics') with urgency and aplomb."

Karen Stephenson, President and CEO of NetForm International, Inc.

"Jensen's right. Employees today look for a company where they can invest their experience, knowledge, time, passion, and generate their best return. And the managers who respond to this new reality with 'extreme leadership' will retain the best, most productive and satisfied employees. This highly readable book will provide insights to anyone who is seeking to lead, not just manage."

Tom Kelly, Vice President, Internet Learning Solutions, Cisco Systems

"No matter how important you think you are, I can guarantee that you will become irrelevant if you fail to read this book. *Work 2.0* puts all leaders and managers on notice, and, more important, focuses attention on the coming workplace revolution. Bill Jensen delivers straight talk about the new work contract everyone must come to grips with, whether you're in the boardroom or the boiler room."

Mark Koskiniemi, Managing Director, Buckman Laboratories Pty Ltd Wagga Wagga, NSW, Australia

"Here's a book with attitude! *Work 2.0* is an attitude adjustment, bringing the business ship back on course — full-steam in a new direction. Bill Jensen is at the helm again with business insights for the corporate realm as well as the nonprofit world. He says everything that matters involves human issues, and I appreciate the course correction."

Mark C. Johnson, Ph.D., Director, National Fund Development, YMCA of the USA

"A preacher from the pulpit once impressed on me that we change ourselves by either 'invitation' or 'situation.' Bill Jensen and *Work 2.0* quickly and insightfully invite us into a new world of thinking about our most precious resource: People. At the same time he doesn't hold back in creating a compelling picture of the situation if we don't listen! To real leaders, *Work 2.0* is our wake-up call!"

Rusty Rueff, Senior Vice President, Human Resources, Electronic Arts

"Bill's first book, *Simplicity,* was mandatory reading for my management team at Oracle University, and we applied its practical concepts to our daily workload. I would have predicted that no one could have authored two successive seminal volumes that captured the 21st century work environment so clearly. I was wrong! *Work 2.0* is extremely applicable to today's volatile climate, both from a work/life balance perspective and from the evolution of a new extreme leadership paradigm. *Work 2.0* will be mandatory reading for both my executive team and my employees.

Dennis F. Bonilla, President and CEO, medsn

"*Work 2.0* captures the core requirement of the new leadership with a simple phrase: 'It's the people, stupid.' Not a new message on its surface. But Bill Jensen's genius in this book is that he delves deep below the surface, showing how the rules of success are changing, how what people need is changing. If you want to be a successful leader in these uncertain times, read and be guided by the kind of clearly elucidated new covenant we've come to expect from Jensen's pen. Inspiring! Practical! Challenging!"

Roger Lewin and Birute Regine,
coauthors of *Weaving Complexity and Business: Engaging the Soul at Work*

"Bill Jensen's new book, *Work 2.0*, is a passionate guidebook for building and keeping a winning team of champions. Much like *Simplicity* provided the tips, tools, and techniques to make work simpler, *Work 2.0* gives leaders the rules, models, and know-how to win the 21st century war for talent."

Janice Duis-Lampert, Director, Organizational Effectiveness, Customer Development Group, Ralston Purina Pet Care

"*Work 2.0* is a must-read for all CEOs and managers. You will discover how much you need to move beyond management philosophies of the past. Bill Jensen teaches us with anecdotes and graceful prose that the foundation of a successful company involves the art of finding and retaining talent. To prevail in this most competitive global economy, entrepreneurs and managers everywhere need to shift to the Work 2.0 model."

Alan Ellman, Founder and Vice Chairman, ScreamingMedia

"This book has an important message for today's leaders. It's no longer sufficient to hire great talent. The question of the day is 'How high is your Return on Talent?' Jensen provides a useful framework for leaders who want to increase their personal impact in this area."

David A. Rodriguez, Ph.D., Senior Vice President, Human Resources, Marriott International, Inc.

work 2.o

work 2.0

Building the Future,
One Employee at a Time

Bill Jensen

PERSEUS PUBLISHING

A Member of the Perseus Books Group

Cataloging-in-Publication Data is available from the Library of Congress
ISBN: 0-7382-0804-3

Perseus Publishing is a member of the Perseus Books Group
Find us on the World Wide Web at http://www.perseuspublishing.com

Perseus Publishing books are available at special discounts for bulk purchases in the U.S. by corporations, institutions, and other organizations.
For more information, please contact the Special Markets Department at the Perseus Books Group, 11 Cambridge Center, Cambridge, MA 02142, or call (800) 255-1514 or (617) 252-5298, or email j.mccrary@perseusbooks.com.

Text art direction by Bill Jensen, design by Aimee Leary/Final Art
Text set in 11 pt. Sabon. Display type, sidebars and tables set in Futura

First paperback printing, December 2002
1 2 3 4 5 6 7 8 9 10—04 03 02

To my son, Ian

Read, every day, something no one else is reading.
Think, every day, something no one else is thinking.
Do, every day, something no one else would be silly enough to do.
Christopher Morley

2.0 contents

work **2.0**

Welcome, extreme leaders.

I am thrilled by the paperback release of *Work 2.0*!
Among other things, it affords me the opportunity to answer
the do-over question: "The past year (...fill in your own
timeframe — month/year/decade...) has been even more
turbulent and uncertain than when this book was first
released. How does that affect the ideas in *Work 2.0*?"

More Timeless Than Ever

We're in the post-everything economy. The heady times are gone.

That's why this is a tough-love book for tough times.
When *2.0* was first released, we were beginning to see headlines
like "Number of Jobless Shoots Up," "Market Hits New Lows,"
and "Surviving The Downturn." Some of today's news is
even bleaker.

That makes the counterpoint — "It's The People,
Stupid!" — even more important. *Work 2.0*'s goal is to
take the People v. Profits debate to a completely new level, by
focusing on timeless values like trust, respect, integrity, fairness,
and accountability. Because no matter happens to the economy,
these things still matter — in fact, they matter even more.

If hindsight were to change anything in this book, I would
place this graphic on every single page: **R-E-S-P-E-C-T.**

1

While I can't sing it or spell it anywhere near as well as Soul Diva Aretha, I can appreciate its importance. From the research behind each of my books, I have learned that most leaders must change how they earn and cultivate respect.

More Timely Than Ever

The destination hasn't changed, but the journey sure has. Today's approaches to trust, respect, and work/life issues are broken, or — at best — badly damaged. It is no longer enough to place survival of the business ahead of fairness, integrity, and accountability. It's no longer enough to relegate people issues to holding hands, singing *Kumbaya* together, saluting the corporate flag, and then expecting everyone to bust their humps even more — either in pursuit of profits, or merely to keep their jobs.

No. The tough economy, the events of September 11th, the layoffs, the scandals, the perp-walks, the vanishing life savings and future opportunities, the lost time with family and kids — not to mention all the "mundane" daily traumas — have forever changed how everyone looks at people issues.

Since *2.0* was first released, I have been on the road talking with thousands of people. Some had lost their jobs. Many were worried about staying employed, about their future, or their retirement income, or their kids' college funds. But what resonated with each of them, and what they repeatedly told me, was that the definition of respect was changing.

More and more, the rules of work are changing how people live their lives. It is no longer acceptable to say that there's *work* and there's *life* and it's up to employees to balance the two.

The hard realities of productivity, efficiency, and bottom-line results are driving how much time and energy we have left over for "soft," personal needs. That's why *Work 2.0* addresses issues like work simplification, worktool usability, leadership skillsets, and more. Because each of them can shift the balance.

To build better workplaces, leaders must first understand

how the design of work impacts the quality of our lives. Those
are the details you will find in *Work 2.0*: changing our lives by
changing the design of work.

Building the Future, One Employee at a Time

Corporate success is now very dependent upon the skills of every
individual in the organization. Successful firms will find that the
future of work is personalized. Tools, goals, and development
will grow even more tailored to each individual.

I know, I know. That's so counterintuitive. "Everybody's
gotta work superhard just to ensure *corporate* success. How
can we, as leaders, shift our focus from that to the needs
of each *individual*? How would that help us survive, grow,
and win?"

Here's how...

Embrace the Asset Revolution. Since the hardcover version
of *2.0* appeared, Watson Wyatt Worldwide came out with a
study of more than 500 firms focused on "human capital
management practices" and "talent acquisition and retention."
(Translation: People Stuff).

They found that superior human capital management is a
leading, rather than a trailing, indicator of improved financial
success. Forty-three of forty-nine key human capital practices
had a positive correlation to improving a company's market
value. How you demonstrate respect for your people — day in,
day out — has become an early-warning system for short-term
and long-term returns.

Work 2.0 shows you where to focus. When you change
how you use people's time, attention, ideas, knowledge, passion,
energy, and social networks, you actively demonstrate respect for
people — and establish the foundation for corporate success.

Build My Work My Way. You've already experienced this shift
with your customers — using mass customization technologies
and other one-to-one approaches. *Fortune* magazine recently
described this new direction: "Managing the enterprise not as

a collection of products and services, not as a group of territories, but as a portfolio of customers."

Work 2.0 says, "Guess what? This is not only a consumer trend. If every worker-bee must continually produce morebetterfaster, you might want to look at how you use one-to-one approaches with your employees too."

If employee choices and actions affect your bottom line, you can't afford not to implement My Work My Way! It's the key to focusing on their personal — not just organizational — productivity.

Deliver Peer-to-Peer Value. Simple fact: The future of your business depends upon how everyone in your firm collaborates. Unfortunate reality: Leaders must do more to add greater value to how their teams work together.

If you are competing in a world where teamwork is the difference between winning and losing, *Work 2.0* invites you to consider the new rules, tools, and best practices that are emerging in the peer-to-peer marketplace.

Develop Extreme Leaders. Leadership mattered yesterday. It will matter tomorrow, and forever. That's timeless.

What's changing is *how* leaders lead. The future of leadership includes greater accountability for performance, with a greater willingness to be challenged on, and address, work-level details.

Scandals and a whole bunch of basic implementation problems have created new calls for *transparency*. This brings us full-circle to "soft" issues like trust and respect. Investors want to see more of the inner workings of your company so they can trust you with their assets, and customers want to see more so they can better track how you keep your promises.

Work 2.0 says, "Be prepared for the *real* change." With business and management practices under greater scrutiny from the outside, your relationship with employees will change too. Even if nobody says it to your face, employees are wondering why they should trust you to manage the assets they supply — time, attention, passion, and more.

Tomorrow's leaders — the ones who survive today's turmoil — will be those who have earned the deep trust and respect of their employees.

One Timeless Idea, Lots of New Accountabilities

With time, we all gain the power of hindsight. If pressed, would I amend any of the key ideas within *Work 2.0*?

Full disclosure: You bet.

I way-underestimated two things:

1) The degree to which the phrase, "control over one's own destiny," had become taboo — associated solely with dot-bomb ventures and a hedonistic go-go economy. While that connection was never my intention, I guess I should have seen it coming.

   But don't let that miscalculation stop you from changing how work gets done, or from reflecting upon what you read. The core idea in this book is just too important:

   Do more to respect each and every individual as you build your business.

   That idea is timeless.

2) I also underestimated the degree to which work has already moved into Version 2.0.

   The future is already here, if we have the will to see it.

Bill Jensen
Bill@Work2.com

PS:

If you have time for only one page in this book, make it page 77.

Fill out the SimplerWork Index survey.

Your answers will drive you into the rest of the book. Guaranteed.

section **1.**

The (Asset) Revolution Begins

*It is no longer acceptable to say that there's **work** and there's **life** and it's up to employees to balance the two.*

No *matter what happens to the economy, timeless values like* **R-E-S-P-E-C-T** *will always matter.*

To build better workplaces,
we must first see
how the design of work
impacts the quality
of our lives.

It's time to take the
**People v. Profits debate
to a new level:**
*by using timeless values,
and by changing
how leaders
design our work.*

chapter 1

Work 2.0

The new contract

> As if you could kill time
> without injuring eternity.
> **Henry David Thoreau**

> To thine own self be true.
> **William Shakespeare**

THE NEW WORK CONTRACT
OUR VIEW, FROM THE WORKFORCE TO LEADERS

A DEAR LEADER:

funny thing happened on the way to the revolution.

Your emphasis on productivity and cost-cutting forced us to change how we think about the war for our talent. For that, we thank you! Your ability to stay focused on the bottom line has inspired us.

We had gotten lazy about controlling our own destiny. We figured if we focused on customers and profits, continuously changed and grew, drank the corporate Kool-aid, and did great work — we'd be the masters of our own fate. Boy, are we glad you woke us from that fairy tale.

So we watched what you do. We studied how you constantly push for greater returns on investment to ensure your own future. Based on what we learned, we have rewritten our work contract. You are not effectively managing the assets we provide, and we're calling you on it.

Decent pay, appropriate benefits, great culture and leadership — all are givens in this contract. Important…but baseline issues. After that, it gets interesting, and personal.

This new covenant between us cuts to the heart of who owns, controls, and sets the rules for productivity. Specifically, how much value you create for us when you organize our work.

It's pretty simple, really. More and more, a big piece of the working capital you leverage to get stuff done is ours. You want us to spend our assets — our time, our attention, our ideas, knowledge, passion, energy, and social networks — on work that you think is important. That means, more and more, we've got to think like investors.

We are students of the marketplace, have learned quickly, and need to audit your efforts: Are you making productive use of our assets? Would an hour invested in a competitor's firm provide a better return? Are you creating better communities than we can find outside in the networked world?

Throw out much of what you thought you knew about creating a "great place to work." A new work contract is hitting your shores. We call this new covenant Work 2.0. Our relationship with you must return more value on our working capital.

Here are the Articles of our new work contract. If you want to attract or keep us, the next step is yours.

The New Coin of the Realm

Article 1.
Our working capital gets stuff done.
You use our assets — time, attention, ideas, knowledge, passion, energy, and social networks — to make your company go. The new contract is all about how to leverage our working capital, and how not to.

Article 2.
Our work is an investment.
Our time and attention are finite, becoming more valuable and sought-after with each tick of the clock. We choose whether to invest our experience, knowledge, passion, and energy and how much to invest. And the social networks we use to get stuff done are the friends and teammates whose trust we have earned. Tell us again: Why should we invest all these assets in you?

Article 3.
We want better returns on our investment.

If an hour invested in your firm could be invested in a competitor for greater return, your best people will leave to make that investment. If you want us to stay with you, here is how we think about ROI:

- How easy it is to make a big impact
- How much of our time is spent doing great and important work
- How much and how fast we learn
- How challenging, rewarding, and exciting our work remains
- How much personal success and balance we achieve — however we choose to define these things
- How well, or poorly, you use the assets we provide

Article 4.
Hello, value — or goodbye.

The idea of getting greater returns on our working capital forces new criteria into the employment contract. You and the company are a middleman between us and our teammates, customers, and the marketplace. Our exit criteria are no longer just warm-and-fuzzy issues like feeling appreciated. Middlemen must add lots of value, or we dump them. Fast.

Article 5.
Productivity is personal.

We know the formula for productivity: Make more at less cost. Here's how it gets applied in our new contract: More personal success — that comes faster and deeper and is more meaningful — with a lot less wasted time and energy. We have very high expectations for how long it takes to see the impact of our work. For every day spent with your company, it must get easier to do great work, make ourselves better, and make the world a better place. Now, that's productivity and efficiency in a knowledge-based economy.

Article 6.
What must radically change is how we use the company to get stuff done.

Your firm is a tool we use to connect with customers and the marketplace. Start acting like an elegant tool. We believe that infrastructure — not just conversation — is part of our dynamic relationship with you. Technology, processes, information flows, and everything that connects us and organizes our work need to change. Change them to meet our needs, just as you currently adapt to meet customer and company needs.

Article 7.
We win, you win, they win.

The New Economy changed the nature of a lot of the work we do — from making things to making choices. More and more, corporate and customer success are tied to the decisions that each of us makes, and how we make them. So if you focus on creating value for us and on how we make decisions, everybody wins! This three-way win is the anchor of the new contract. We're no fools. We've designed this covenant to ensure that our workplace enhances our ability to satisfy corporate and customer needs. Pay attention to what we can teach you about that workplace, and we'll help you keep your job longer too!

Article 8.
Results follow passion.

If you want faster innovation and productivity from us, listen to what we're passionate about. Listen to what rocks our heart, what inspires and excites us. Ask and listen first, and then set your targets, goals, and plans. We'll exceed them every time.

Article 9.
The important fundamentals haven't changed.

None of this changes the basics: decent pay, appropriate benefits, being on a winning team with great people, great leaders, and great communication. These are the foundation you need to build upon.

Creating Value for Us

Article 10.
Work 2.0 value is My Work My Way.

More and more, the best places to work will be those that tailor work to who we are as unique individuals. We are business units of one. We all may win together, but the speed, effectiveness, efficiency, and productivity of the team are built upon what each individual brings to the effort. The great places to work will set new standards in real-time responsiveness, interactivity, customization, and personalization.

Article 11.
Work 2.0 value is peer-to-peer connections that deliver personal freedom, growth, and success.

Every day, the networked marketplace makes it easier and cheaper for us to connect with great teammates and amazing people who care about the same things we do — who are handling the same challenges, at the same time. We're beyond comparing the culture of Company A and Company B. We scrutinize how you build teams and communities according to our personal standards. If your social networks and peer-to-peer connections are better than any we could experience without you, that's value.

Article 12.
Work 2.0 value is more useful, usable, and practical tools than we could build ourselves.

The marketplace is creating awesome informational and productivity tools. As consumers, we can get the information we need to make decisions, tailored to our needs, easily and cheaply. With our friends and families, we are building new ways to exchange ideas, information, and decisions that would blow your mind — and those experiences outside the workplace are changing what we expect from you. Value, to us, comes from tools that are better than what we could build or buy ourselves.

Article 13.
Work 2.0 value is now, wow, and addictive learning.

We'll go wherever we get just-in-time, on-demand learning
that's exciting and continually draws us back for more. And
where leaders create the space and time to think — sometimes
slowing things down enough for what we're learning to sink
in. The "wow" part comes from connecting with, and learning
from, great people — not from technology. No boundaries exist
between play and work, informal and formal learning, tasks
and what we need to know. We can find this in the outside,
networked world. What are we finding inside your company?

Article 14.
Work 2.0 changes what you value, and therefore what you measure.

Work 1.0 valued speed, teamwork, diversity, creativity,
innovation, etc. as the foundations of productivity and
performance. Great! Don't lose those! We'll build upon them.
But Work 2.0 goes further:

- Do you consider the respectful use of your employees'
  time to be an organizational value?
- Do you measure the usability of the tools you
  build for us?
- Do you even understand how we need to learn, the
  information we need, and how we need it?

If you want your company to be productive, you must start
changing what you measure and where you place the highest
value.

Article 15.
Work 2.0 forever changes how our work is evaluated.

Truly talented people are not driven to please authority figures.
The people you most want to keep seek satisfaction through the
work itself. Since the ultimate arbiter of whether our work
produces something of value is the customer and the marketplace,

the evaluations, reviews, and recognition we most value come from peers, customers, and competitors who are closest to our work. We'll hang with them our whole lives. Odds are, we'll work with you for only a limited time.

Article 16.
Work 2.0 flows from simplicity and common sense.
We will always invest our time, attention, knowledge, passion, and energy in whatever and whoever makes the investment easiest. Common sense governs our choices, not corporate logic. We tolerate management's logic, but act on our own conclusions. We want to work with and for companies that set new standards in simplicity and commonsenseness.

Article 17.
Work 2.0 ignores timebandits.
Time and attention are the scarcest resources we have. We get ticked off when they are wasted. Anything, or anyone, inside your organization that wastes our time is likely to be ignored.

Article 18.
Work 2.0 has a great sense of humor.
As individuals, we laugh easily and deeply. Lots of times, at ourselves. Does your firm? Do you? If you can't laugh, you can't learn.

Article 19.
Work 2.0 creates new levels of trust, clarity, and deep conversation.
What will happen when you use our working capital more wisely? We will have more time to connect with the real, wonderful people in your organization. And to talk about stuff that really matters. Deep diversity (of people and ideas) matters. Creativity matters. Changing the world matters. Truth, integrity, and trust matter.

Article 20.
Work 2.0 value starts with me.

We accept personal accountability. Regardless of what our firms do or don't do, we can do more to value other people's working capital. We're accountable for:

- Listening, probing, and understanding what would help those around us to work smarter

- Using other people's time and attention wisely

- Sharing ideas in a more human voice, with more empathy

- Competing on clarity: creating more meaning-making and sense-making around us, and continuously looking at things from the customer's perspective

- Being more impatient as we see companies waste people's potential

- Taking a stand. And having fun. Every day

And, if you do step up to this new contract, we are accountable for:

- Retooling ourselves even faster and more often than we do today

- Helping to create the structure and connections that ensure that our customers and our company succeed

- Helping to ensure that every person around us can fulfill more of his/her own potential

- Asking ourselves: Have I got what it takes today?

- Kicking butt in all competitive situations!

- Revising the "us" and "you" tone of this contract. Fulfilled, this contract transforms all of us into leaders

Contract Decoder: Leader's Guide

This contract is not just some manifesto screaming at leaders, including you, to get a clue. (Although that is among the criteria!)

Consider the themes that run through this new contract: Productivity. Innovation. Speed. Ease of execution. Making a difference. Satisfying customers. Learning. And lots more. Parts of this new covenant between employee and employer read like a leader's fantasy come true. It's all about completely new competitive opportunities, reduced costs, more profits, and more success for your organization.

For the first time since we entered a knowledge and service economy, employees are proposing a work contract that any leader could love. With one big, hairy exception...

Holding You Accountable to Your Own Rules
The people you most want to attract and retain are bringing with them never-seen-before levels of sophistication and insights about the design of knowledge work. They know more than most leaders about how to collaborate, how to organize information, how to communicate, and how decision making really works.

This is because you are hiring them from a networked world. Technology, marketplace, and societal changes are training them to think differently and demand more. They have the devices and the savvy to connect with anybody, anywhere — constantly discovering ways to outwit any Big Brother. As consumers, they have figured out that customized interactions can be a very good thing, providing exactly what they need to make decisions. And they are discovering that one person can quickly and easily mobilize entire communities and social networks.

Sure, a tough economy is — once again — changing the rules, relationships, and covenants between people and organizations. Job seekers and switchers are feeling a hefty dose of tough love. But don't for a minute believe that's the only force driving employee behaviors and career moves. What hasn't changed is that, based on what they've learned outside in the networked world, employees are developing new views on personal productivity, efficiency, and the performance of knowledge work.

They are not caving. They are pushing standards for performance back atcha. Essentially, holding you accountable to your own rules about getting better returns on investments. Only this time, the assets are theirs.

New rules for tough times. Turnabout is fair play. From this point forward, the new war for talent is about personal returns on investments, and the value you place on the assets that people bring with them to work.

Let the battles for talent begin....

chapter 2

Leaders and Managers

What this means to you

Governments...deriv[e] their just powers
from the consent of the governed.
Thomas Jefferson et al.

Labor is...the means of production.
Karl Marx

*T*he choice is yours.

INNOVATE OR FACE DEFEAT

You can keep struggling with all the gyrations in the war for talent — engaging in new skirmishes with each defection or round of layoffs that forces you to lose momentum. Or you can change the rules.

More than ever, the new rules of engagement are being set by the people you want to hire and keep. Not with "pay me this" or "cover such-and-such benefit." But by pressing completely new levels of sophistication and insights on how work gets done.

There is a great and grave difference between employee satisfaction and satisfying employees' workneeds. The new contract and this book are about that difference.

We will not spend much time on compensation, benefits, flextime, making nice to your employees, and the like. All the usual workplace satisfaction criteria — these, and any others you could list — remain as critical as ever. But they are not where the *new* war for talent will be fought. The people you most want to hire and keep are changing the rules of productivity. How good are you at *not* wasting an individual's precious assets as he or she presses to be more efficient and effective?

It's time for the creative destruction of your current approach and a new relationship with the people you wish to lead.

Especially after the economy plummeted in 2001, many of you are too focused on the idea that management, with the economy as enforcer, is in control over who stays and who leaves your company. This book's message: Rip up your beliefs and practices before somebody else does — because it's gonna happen anyway.

Who will shatter those beliefs? The people who are about to walk out your door. And those you're about to hire. That's who.

Here they come....

The Emperor's New Clock

In September 2000, I discovered a rip in the conventional work contract. Six months into an economic downturn, which supposedly forced all employees to do a lot more genuflecting and ring-kissing, an interesting shift in the relationship between employer and employee became clear.

It was during one of those senior executive junkets. You know the kind: exclusive attendance (a "CEO Summit"), great location (chi-chi retreat in California's wine country), great playtime (one-on-one lessons from a world-renowned croquet champion while sipping some of the best wines in the world), and a few outsiders (ahem) to help the attendees look at their navels and think big, important thoughts.

In addition to talking about simplicity and the creation of simpler companies, I presented a few pages from what would become this book. "There are four trends that are very important to your future," I cautioned. But, because I was still making sense of these trends, I left lots of wiggle room as to how and when: "They may change how you lead sometime within the next five years or so."

The first people to come up to me after the presentation were the CEO and executive vice president from a firm in the field of life science. (They've asked to remain nameless. You'll see why in a moment.) The CEO said, "I've gotta tell ya, you were wrong about something."

My heart sank...until he finished his thought. "One of those trends — leadership being accountable for wasting people's time, or using it wisely — is dead-on. What's off is your timing. Leadership accountability is not five or more years in the future, it's now. We just parted company with our president for this reason."

He continued, "The people we've hired won't tolerate anyone or anything that wastes their time. Because the president didn't get that, we were about to lose some very talented employees — like our director of marketing. That loss would've been bigger than losing a president. So the president is gone."

Whoa.

Could this occur at your company? Is it just an isolated blip that happened to some poor schmuck-of-a-leader, or could it happen to you?

Admittedly, in both booming and tough times, this type of employee brinkmanship is rare. Yet...see it for what it is: a warning shot across leadership's bow. The signs are there, and they are screaming, "Pay attention! Listen. Learn. Change."

The Making of the New Contract

Your workforce knows that they have to be more productive, more efficient, and deliver morebetterfaster every day. That's not news. What is different is that they are pushing back — seeking new proof, information, commitments, and measurable standards about *how* that's going to happen. These are the first acts of an emerging new contract.

Even if your company is currently ranked as a great place to work, watch out. Today's economy — boom, bust, or somewhere in between — is still a knowledge economy. As such, labor is realizing that they own the means to your production. They're figuring out that you derive the power to get stuff done through their consent. You don't empower them. They empower you, and your company, your plans, your strategies.

Your key talent are demanding proof that you value their resources — appreciating that their time, attention, current skills, energy, and all the social connections they leverage in the name of business results are precious and limited. They also want proof that their unlimited resources — ideas, knowledge, future skills, and passion — will be put to immediate use and will make a real difference. Unlike anything you've seen before, the terms of this contract are about personal effectiveness, not entitlement.

The good news is that as you get better at leveraging your employees' working capital, everybody wins. Increased individual productivity affects team effectiveness, efficiency, creativity, and organizational alignment. That affects company innovation, and productivity, and truly connects your people and your customers.

More on that later. Let's come back to the forces that sank our poor ex-president.

Where did this new contract come from? Is the previous chapter just some whining manifesto tacked to the wall, bellowing at you to "get a clue"? No.

Is the new covenant between employer and employee just about more compensation, stock options, benefits, day-care centers, or foosball tables in the lounge? Is it solely the domain of dot-coms, the under-25 crowd, or a blow-your-socks-off bull economy? No, nope, and definitely not.

When I look back over more than a decade of research, studying how almost a thousand companies design work, I find a new level of sophistication among the workforce.

Yes, they still crave to be in a great place to work. That means they still want you to create a culture of participation, demonstrating great teamwork and flexibility. Yes, they still want you to have learning and development strategies, coaching, mentoring, and great communication in place to support and develop people. And, yes, they still want be on a winning team that's achieving great results.

But they're also being more particular, deliberate, and discerning in their search for greater work value. They want to know what value you add as a middleman between them and their customers, between them and their tasks. For example:

Are your tools, processes, and information flows user-centered? (Extremely valuable.) Or are they designed to make it easier for you to manage your employees? (Of dubious value to them.)

Having read the new contract, you know that focusing on work value is all about delivering better results to the customer and company.

But, in times of wrenching change, knowledge workers need more control over how they have an impact, more control over their *personal* productivity. During tough economic times, even more so. Your employees are acutely aware that their future is on the line every day. They'll deliver the results. But they also want greater control over their own destiny.

WIIFM?
(What's In It for Me?)

You *bought* this book as a businessperson. You wanted to learn more about the war for talent, the new contract, simpler workdays, corporate survival, whatever.

I hope you *read it* as a person.

As a businessperson, you know you've got to rely increasingly on the people around you. Everything's changing so fast and with such intensity that if you are going to succeed, you've got to find better ways to unleash the potential of everyone in your organization. That's the goal of the new contract: taking your workplace to a new level...to Work 2.0.

But as a person, like the refrigerator-door wisdom says, you're not gonna lie on your deathbed wishing you had spent more time at work. You want to leave behind something that really mattered. Not just business results.

If you're like most leaders, at the core of what matters are your personal passions, vision, and values. Hopefully, one of those values is an unshakeable and unquestionable respect for others. That's where you and this book intersect.

Work 2.0 places before you a simple self-assessment question: "As a leader, am I changing enough to demonstrate that I respect and trust the people around me?"

The question may be simple: Are you keeping up with the rate of change? The answers are not.

What leaders must do to demonstrate deep respect and trust for people is ramping up daily. It's no longer just during facetime or while being sensitive to "soft" issues.

Proof of respect now includes, among other things, your ability to build user-centered infrastructures and deliver just-in-time, on-demand information to frontline decision makers. Proof of trust now includes the willingness to have your views challenged and changed from the bottom up, because many people closest to the work know more about efficiency and productivity than you do.

The workforce has watched how you focus on returns on investment. They are doing the same thing. From this point forward, R-E-S-P-E-C-T includes better use of the assets the workforce brings with them. They want less wasted time, energy, and talent. And better returns on those assets.

That's gonna take more than making sure people feel appreciated and telling them that the work they do is important. You need to change your plans, focus, and priorities fast enough so that the infrastructures you build, the hierarchies you establish, the tools you create — everything that they use to get work done — demonstrate that you respect their time, attention, and energy.

Whew! Living up to refrigerator-door ideals just got a whole lot tougher and more complicated! Suddenly, "Am I changing enough?" takes on a whole new, chilling aura.

Work 2.0 is for leaders who believe that even under these new conditions, demonstrating respect and trust in others will always bring greater personal and business rewards.

Your WIIFM: This book is a tool for figuring out new ways to interweave your personal values with doing what it takes to succeed. You'll encounter guiding principles, getting-started tips, and stories from those who have begun their Work 2.0 journey.

Whether you change enough to live those values is up to you.

The Four Horsemen of the Coming Creative Destruction

Why we're going to have to change how we work. During the coming decade, every company that is heavily dependent upon knowledge or service workers for growth and productivity will have to reinvent how it attracts and retains those people. The new great places to work will anticipate four forces of change coming their way and get ahead of them.

These forces will create ever-increasing accountabilities for you and your company:

1. Asset Revolution
New ways of thinking; a wake-up call for leaders

2. My Work My Way
New accountabilities for personal productivity

3. Peer-to-Peer Value
New accountabilities for teamwork and collaboration

4. Extreme Leadership
New accountabilities if you are to live your personal values

If you don't reinvent your current ways of doing things, your employees and the economy will do it for you. These forces will drive you much closer to frontline work than you've been in years.

1 Work 2.0 Is an Asset Revolution

If there's anyone who knows about focusing on the work, it's Janine Bay. She's director of vehicle customization at Ford Motor Company. Even today, female engineers are rare in the auto industry. Janine was blowing the doors off the competition as the chief engineer on the Ford Mustang during the mid-seventies, when quality really was Job One.

"I'm old," she says with a bit of self-deprecating humor. "After 25 years, the golden handcuffs are clamped solidly on me. But the people I mentor have a very different approach to life."

She continues, "I just talked last week to a young man who said, 'Janine, I appreciate all your help, but I don't think I can do it anymore. I'm outta here.' He's a Ph.D. He's 27.

"And even in a tough economy, he can pretty much go anywhere, anytime. He said to me, 'I'm not here because of the money. Quite frankly, I've been offered a lot more money than I get here.' He said what matters to him most is whether his work is making a difference, his own pride in the quality of that work, whether he is appreciated, and how quickly he can take himself to new levels.

"I can understand where he's coming from," says Bay. "Way back when, I was one of the rebels in the company who decided that I really needed to diversify my portfolio of experiences if I ever was going to get anywhere. Which, in the early to mid-eighties, was a very controversial approach to career management. Now I'm seeing a lot more willingness to cut and run if that portfolio isn't top priority for management. And not just a spoken priority; leaders have to be super fast in whatever we do to help build that personal portfolio."

Tables get turned. Your incessant push for short-term business results has made a lasting impression. Let's be honest. Your expectations are never in the distant future. You expect quarterly, monthly, weekly, daily, and in some cases, hourly results.

Ironically, the killer employees who are most responsive to that pressure now have the same short-term expectations of their investments in you. Quid pro quo, babe.

You leverage assets to get stuff done. So do they. On your books, you can depreciate assets. Each day, your employees are realizing that they are being forced to depreciate hours and knowledge wasted within your organization. They want fewer write-offs and more, better, faster returns on what they bring to the party.

As you continue to cut costs and people, the ones who are left are beginning to figure out that you just redefined "working capital." You're now including, and counting on, the assets they bring to you.

Some of the questions you'll face in the coming war for talent:

- "How much of my time is spent doing great work?"
- "Show me how you put teams together. How good are you at community-building?"
- "Is my manager smarter, better, faster than I am? Does he or she have the skills to help me be my best? And have *my* needs in mind, not just the company's? If not, find me one who does. Now."
- "Show me how your company is respectful of my time. And I don't mean sending me home at five, or generous vacations. Show me how your systems and structures are designed for my use, not just yours."
- "Do you do usability testing on the information flows and tools you build for me? If not, why not?"
- "How much and how fast can I learn in this environment?"
- "Will I get to work on what I'm passionate about?"
- "How nice that you communicate so much. Now: Can I get the exact information I need, how I need it, when I need it, and without you living in spin?"

In their own words. Tiffanie Lopatin is a professional poacher. As executive talent recruiter at Bank of America, she's on the prowl for your best talent. She reports, "I go after passive job seekers. They're not looking. I seek them out, usually outside of our industry. During 2001, I saw a dramatic rise in pushbacks and qualifiers from people who did decide to join us. They really asserted themselves. I've heard things like, 'I'm a virtual worker,

I can be global, why do I have to move where you want me to go?'"

Typical of the asset revolution is this exchange relayed by Lopatin....

"I surfaced one woman who was such solid A-talent, I felt we just had to find a place for her. She came in for an exploratory interview. Boy, did she push back! She asked detailed questions about her potential job, who communicates with whom, how different departments relate, and who shared

The Hairball from Hell

Are you choking on the new contract's use of "working capital"? If so, the idea is doing its job. It got your attention.

Well-intentioned academics and consultants coined terms that would not trouble you. Like "human capital" for people and their skills. "Intellectual capital" for what they know and share. And "social capital" for how and why they work together.

Sure, these are very important ideas. But they're so...*sanitary*...and they promote an illusion that this capital is yours to manage.

Anyone who sweats on a loading dock, pulls an all-nighter writing computer code, holds the hand of a sick patient, or trains salespeople will gladly shatter this illusion for you.

New view of working capital: Workers choose how to invest their assets — time, attention, energy, etc. — to get stuff done. Academic frameworks can no longer hide the fact that these are assets you covet, yet employees choose how, when, and if to invest them. The more you cut costs, the more you're using their assets as capital to meet your current obligations.

That may not jibe with how your CFO defines working capital. Doesn't matter. As University of Kentucky chancellor Otis Singletary said: "Whatever people think, is."

Making the mental leap and grappling with this new definition are important. The leap will bring you closer to what the 21st-century war for talent is all about.

what information. And after that first day, three different hiring managers were interested in her.

"By the time I called her with the news, she had pulled out. She said, 'You're a great company. You care more about customer needs than most firms I've met. I wish I could work for you. But these positions are only going to utilize skills I've already got. They're not going to help me grow at the rate I need to grow.'

"The story has a happy ending, though, because we created a bigger position for her. I'm very proud of the bank for coming up with a win/win solution. But we're going to have to keep coming up with tailored solutions! In the past year, every A-level offer has consistently involved customizing the position or the work itself."

Here's a sampling of other people who think and act the same way, in organizations like yours. (By the way, each of these individuals has been fast-tracked within their companies. They are involved in leadership development activities, and — solely for short-term economic reasons — are temporarily hanging in there with their current employers.)

Employees expect short-term results too: Quid pro quo, babe

- From a middle manager in one of the world's largest energy companies, who momentarily lost it, expressing what many top performers are feeling:

  "I walk into this IT meeting. They were having some argument about Net Meeting [an online collaboration tool] — how they couldn't get it to work. I stood up and said, 'What is wrong with you people? My family has run Net Meeting out of our garage for a year. We don't have the resources that [this company] has, nor do we have a gigantic IT department to help us do it. What's your problem?!'"

- From a talented MBA who is building tomorrow's Internet and has job-hopped through her still-young career: "More and more truly gifted people around me are being turned off. This little flame ignites in each of my teammates, and then something happens in the company that smashes it, totally. High performers have a very low tolerance level for that kind of crap. Once or twice…well, that's just part of life. More than a few times…we're outta there. Life's too short."

- From a mid-manager at a telecommunications company — someone who fully understands the value of her own working capital and what's happening to her industry:

Can you say "business units of one"?

"I am struck by how little value corporations place on our time. I focus on three things when I evaluate how my time gets spent: (1) How much impact am I having? (2) Am I constantly learning? (3) Is my work interesting? If the answers are not extremely positive, it's costing me way too much to work here."

Welcome to the Asset Revolution. Be honest: You want to tap into the marrow of your talent's humanity. You want to leverage their ability to imagine, create, judge, and build relationships. OK — they're up for it. But what do they get in return?

The next level in the war for talent is an asset revolution. This includes how leadership creates daily/weekly/monthly/quarterly returns for the people you employ.

Get ready to talk about a different kind of ROI. If it's true that the best approach is to hire for attitude and train for skill, prepare yourself for an investor's attitude.

The expectations are real. They are not going away.

2
Work 2.0 Is My Work My Way

The future of work is personalized and tailored. Can you say, "business units of one"? Disruption is coming like you've never seen before.

Sound like too much loss of control? Get over it.

Sound too complicated and like too much work for you? Welcome to the real world of work. Life's tough. Get a helmet.

Does My Work My Way sound anti-team to you? Great teams and totally collaborative environments require each individual to bring more to the party, and change more than ever before. This increased personalization is what's required if you expect employees to commit to enhanced preparation and self-improvement, carrying one's own weight, and contributing as much to the team as possible.

The very nature of knowledge work — interconnected out the wazoo, increasingly complex, with volume and velocity of choices, information, partners, and challenges all on steroids — is leaping past *anyone's* ability to build teams, align visions, or create best practices fast enough. One of the punchlines from my previous book, *Simplicity*, is even more true today: Work complexity is *the* productivity issue for the coming decade.

Tom Petzinger, author of *The New Pioneers*, who has spent years studying and reporting on frontline heroics, had this to say in *Simplicity*: "The obstacle is not the ability or willingness of people to engage as fully committed knowledge workers. To seek, think, and create are human traits. The challenge is how management chooses to focus people's time and energy."

Most companies are still in the Neanderthal Age when it comes to their ability to truly help individuals work smart enough, fast enough. The research behind *Simplicity* found that few organizations have figured out how to focus people's time and energy by getting employees what they need to get the work done. All the great collaboration and teamwork we crave also hides a dirty little management secret: Most companies are not delivering tools, information, and support in ways that individuals find useful, and they're relying on teams to make up for this shortcoming.

The new frontier. "Five years from now, we will have failed as leaders if we have not addressed these issues!" says an impassioned Michael Volkema, CEO of furniture-maker Herman Miller. "There must be a new level of commitment and sophistication around meeting each individual's needs."

Volkema has an interesting leadership challenge. His predecessor, Max DePree, son of the founder of Herman Miller, wrote the book (quite literally) on leading in completely new ways. While Volkema is proud that Herman Miller has been ranked among "America's Most Admired Companies" 15 of the first 16 times those kudos were awarded, and 5th among the "100 Best Corporate Citizens" in America, he sees the need to take the company to the next level.

"People who are much more scholarly than I," Volkema says humbly, "are connecting the dots between these trends: We're facing 10 to 15 years of skilled labor shortages, globally. There are underlying disruptive sets of technologies entering our lives, at ever-increasing rates. And, across all industries, new knowledge workers will not be frustrated by lack of opportunity, but by having too many opportunities.

"Our research and design teams are heavily involved in rethinking the very nature of work. We're on the threshold of a networked economy where we must add much more value to people who are trying to connect with each other and with new information." Volkema concludes: "Greater ability to leverage one's own team and community is critical, obvious, and gets all the press. The new frontier is enhancing individual freedom and control over their work. The challenge for many companies will be in how to do that while delivering the necessary business results."

The coming changes. Here is a small sampling of My Work My Way developments (My-Way, for short) *already* underway in companies like yours. There are case studies and stories about changes like these throughout this book:

- Cafeteria-based compensation plans are coming. The employer offers a mix base, bonus, and equity. Within given parameters, employees pick the percentages of each that best meet their personal or family needs
- Employees are pushing back on the design of enterprise portals, the entryway to a company's databases and intranet. (There's still too little control over what information they get and how they get it)
- Daily meeting agendas are being designed based on the needs of employees
- Employees are signing written agreements that specify how virtual they can be so they can take control of their worklife
- Mini "drop-in centers" are being built in highly congested regions. Goal: Commute less and drop in for high-speed social and network connections
- Herman Miller is even looking into individual climate control! Hot, cold, and just right is coming to cubeville

In a time warp? If employee-centric ideas like these seem foreign to you, or if you imagine employees getting a better hold of their worklife through flextime, worklife programs, opportunities to participate, and the like — that's so 1980s. Welcome to the early 21st century, a Work 2.0 world.

But don't for a minute think that My-Way is about creating an entitlement cookie jar. This is *all* about personal productivity. All about getting closer to the customer. All about getting exponentially more done every day, with exponentially less time to get it done.

I would be yanking your chain if I said the only way to deliver great results is to focus on My-Way. It's not. Great teamwork; focused, passionate leaders and clear goals are irreplaceable. However, the whole My-thing *is* supercritical if you want to deliver those results *and* compete in the new war for talent.

Same values, new standards. "We don't do a lot of fancy My-Way stuff yet," says Hans Eisenman, head of Employee Tools and Systems for Earthlink, an Internet provider. "But even the most basic things we do — like making it easier for HR and managers to do salary adjustments and transfers over the Web — are the precursors and the foundation for a different way of working. Customization is the future of work. For one core reason — to make it easier and faster to get closer to the customer."

Eisenman's pace quickens as he talks about his role in helping 6,400 people do their jobs. His passion reflects the most critical component of My-Way: company values. Eisenman's dedication to changing the design of work is utterly consistent with Earthlink's company values.

"We have ten core values at Earthlink. The first one is, 'We respect the individual, and believe that individuals who are treated with respect and given responsibility respond by giving their best.' We really live that here. I think My Work My Way is the way people do want to work. Most people want to be trusted. They want to be in an environment where tailored and personalized worktools and structures prove that they can be trusted."

Respect. Trust. What's really important about My-Way is that in a Work 2.0 world, the bar is being raised for what you have to deliver when you say you trust and respect people.

Eisenman continues: "Our founder, Sky Dayton, says that Earthlink is about removing time and space from communication. I believe that's my role too. In real time, I've got to get people what they want and need to satisfy our customers. That also means we have to get really, really good at knowing what people want and need. Technology doesn't answer that question for us. Our core value about respect does. It continually drives us to learn more and more about our employees' changing needs."

Know me. Know my work. Know what I need. Know how to help me.

Most companies suck at this. Work 2.0 workers will not tolerate this shortcoming. They want customized work experiences. They deserve customized experiences.

Which brings us to the lies and truths we've been telling ourselves for the past couple of decades. The basic truth is that managers and coaches will always be the most crucial source for know-me, know-how-to-help-me customized interaction. The big lie is that companies are actually doing enough to develop the frontline and mid-level managers who can address employee work needs. For the most part: Ain't happenin'.

Oh, sure, all the biggie companies have coaching, mentoring, and development efforts for their managers. But their (well-intentioned) efforts either lack the necessary discipline to have the desired impact or, worse, are stuck in a Work 1.0 world.

One team, new assumptions. Even in the most impassioned, the-team-is-everything environment, you must start with the assumption that everyone needs to be in control of their own destiny.

With just one sentence, Rusty Rueff demonstrates the quantum leap most companies are going to have to make if they want Work 2.0 employees to trust them.

Rueff is the head of Human Resources at Electronic Arts (EA), the world's largest video-games company. He's in charge of ensuring that EA's great culture and passionate people are the core of their competitive advantage.

We were discussing the vision/mission thing. Rueff jumped in with, "I'm constantly sitting down with people, saying, 'Let's talk about the big picture...'"

Now, how do you think the overwhelming majority of managers in most companies have been trained to complete that sentence? Describing the big picture probably covers global market forces, or the company's goals or values, or customer needs, or the bottom-line, or teamwork, blahblahblah...right?

Here's how Rueff completes it: "Let's talk about the big picture. Let's talk about where you are going."

180° shift. "People need to be in control of their own destiny. If I come in with corporate thinking, they tune it out. But if I can dial it back into, 'Let's talk about you, and let's talk about how you fit into what we're all trying to get done together,' all the cynicism goes away." Rueff concludes, "We are teaching every single one of our managers to do that."

In an economy that provides more choices and challenges than how-to's, an individual's need to have greater control over his or her own destiny is a force that will not be denied. *That* is the spirit and guiding principle behind My Work My Way.

3
Work 2.0 Is Peer-to-Peer Value

Boasting of an open, sharing, and collaborative environment nowadays is like saying, "We're a great place to work. We provide air for our employees to breathe! Flushable toilets too!"

P2P 2U: Open and sharing...Been there. Done that. What have you done for us lately?

If you want to maximize what your people can accomplish, you're going to have to take peer-to-peer (P2P) interaction to new places. P2P guru Alan Ellman recounts how this kind of higher calling found him: "I got home one day, and there's a message on my machine. Something about American Express and 'Call me about an important matter.' I thought maybe something happened to my card.

"It ended up that Jim Robinson, former CEO of Amex, was looking to put some money into an emerging company," says Ellman, founder of Screaming Media. "He hooked me up with Jay Chiat [Chairman of Screaming Media, founder of Chiat/Day Advertising], who is an amazing guy. He loves inspiring people like me to do things that are not in their comfort zone. I used to be a computer hacker. Now I run a global sense-making business."

Leadership: Jumping the Chasm

Work 1.0	**Work 2.0**
Organizational productivity	Personal productivity
Operational excellence	Radical simplicity: Focusing on what people need
Operational consolidation	Consolidate processes and structure, but people are business units of one
Respect, Trust, Integrity 1.0: How people are treated	Respect, Trust, Integrity 2.0: How people *and* their assets are treated
Emperor's New Clothes	Emperor's New Clock
Business sophistication pushed down	Work sophistication pushed up

Screaming Media feeds custom-filtered, real-time content to corporate and news clients. Their technology works in the background to continually search millions of items and feed you only what matches your profile. That way you and your team can share information in ways and at speeds that were never before possible. Screaming Media marries the disciplines of My-Way customization and creating P2P value.

But, frankly, their techno-specifics, or anyone's, are not what makes the P2P story so new and challenging. It's how rapidly what is valued in peer-to-peer exchanges can shift, and how much your employees can teach you about those shifts.

The standards are changing. Collaboration, teamwork, learning, and communities are leaping to completely new places — often, way beyond corporate leadership's endorsements, assistance, sponsorship, and funding. From better-informed grapevines (like F**kedCompany.com and WorkingWounded.com), to information architecture and content management (like Screaming Media), to totally user-centered sharing spaces (like Groove or Topica), to just-in-time, on-demand learning, and much more, new frontiers in how people connect with each other are being crossed daily. Creating a collaborative culture is no longer enough. The future of great places to work will be determined by the ways in which a company delivers value to those interactions.

This means expanding your view of how you add value. Do you know what to do that would save people time every single day? Do you know what to do to enhance trust and relationships between people? Conversely, do you fully understand how you destroy trust and relationships in the way you currently create structures, controls, and communication? Do you know how to get out of the way, and still lead?

Technology may occasionally look like the key driver. It's not. What matters is your willingness to invest in peer-to-peer collaboration in ways that your employees define as valuable, and in ways you never have before.

Setting standards without you. There is only one way you are going to keep succeeding. You need more from all the teamwork within your organization. More innovation. More productivity. More self-direction. Success no longer comes from the top down. It comes from how good you are at finding, funding, focusing, and caring for all the work that bubbles up from below.

The New Economy is finally catching up with the average knowledge worker's need to come up with all those ideas and faster ways to get stuff done. From cell phones, to learning portals, to handheld PDAs, to the Internet's most basic killer app — email — and lots more, it is now easier and cheaper for workers to learn from others, to share, and to grow.

New standards now include what content is most valued, and what social connections, timing, tips and tools, amount of detail versus context setting, and type of coaching are best. All those standards, and more, are being set in today's peer-to-peer connections.

And here's the most important part: All without you!

The new standard-setters. Heath Row is developing and mentoring many of your new employees. Never heard of this guy whose name sounds like an airport? His title is Social Capitalist. He founded and coordinates *Fast Company*'s global readers' network, the Company of Friends. He helps folks develop and coach others, most often by connecting them to other people. This self-described yenta helps people — including the employee standing outside your door right now — learn how to get the most from their boss, and how to maximize their peer-to-peer efforts.

Rachel Chou, an ex-teacher, is now executive producer at Scholastic.com. She is also a new mother. Through iVillage, an online community, she found fellow new moms. They taught each other. They coached each other. They stay connected because they're facing the exact same challenges at the exact time in their kids' life cycles. She has lived the process of building and sustaining community value. She has new

Nobody needs companies anymore to help them collaborate

appreciation and expectations of what that value looks like. She now expects the same standards for community-building at her workplace.

If you want to be a valued middleman between your employees and their work, you are going to have to understand how peers *really* connect with each other to get things done.

Jennifer Corriero (21 years old), and Michael Furdyk (19; founded his first of several companies at 16) are creating new kinds of global leaders through TakingITGlobal. Their Toronto-based, nonprofit organization connects and mentors youth in over 70 countries.

Says Furdyk: "As youth, our greatest fear is not that we are inadequate. It is that we are powerful beyond measure. The biggest shift in the next few years will be in how leaders lead. Companies need to be much more accepting of individuals who don't want to lose their power by being too tied to one company.

"At TakingITGlobal, we're doing our small part to help create those kinds of leaders by demonstrating what happens when they bypass normal channels and connect directly with each other." This includes connecting Ezekial Annan from Ghana with Lena Anastasiades from Cyprus so that she can share what she learned at the Global Knowledge Conference in Kuala Lumpur.

Think about Joree Jacobs and Sami Shelnick when you think about how you'll cut through the clutter caused by intense P2P collaboration. These eighth graders at Nordonia Hills School in Northfield, Ohio, are representative of tomorrow's digital workers. They giggle as they describe how they do their homework together: "While my homework's on my screen," says Sami, "I'm talking to Joree, and IM-ing [instant messaging] Shannon and Jinny, all at the same time." They also report that their teacher's use of PowerPoint is "sooooo b-o-r-i-n-g!"

During this quick tour of P2P advances, I didn't once mention the impact of wireless or mobile communications. Like what Joree's peer, Yuriko, is up to in Japan. 95 percent of all Japanese teenage girls have one or more cell phones.[1] Or how Heath Row will soon have greater access to your employees than you do. Or how hundreds of thousands of protesters in Manila organized the ouster of Philippine president Estrada through instant messages broadcast to cell phones. You don't even want to think about some of those stories....

The common thread? In the outside world — where employees escape to when they're not in their cubes — the standards for what's valued and valuable in peer-to-peer connections are ratcheting up. This force of creative destruction is a perfect storm. The Net and other communication technologies have created an unstoppable energy — it keeps getting easier for people to connect with, and learn from, each other in ways that they highly value.

The bottom line for P2P. Your company may serve a critical marketplace or customer need. But nobody needs companies anymore to help them collaborate, share, or create. People can now self-organize amazingly well, thank you. Their daily challenge is to get the most out of each connection, often in the least amount of time.

Throughout this book, you'll find stories about organizations that are tackling this challenge. Cisco, Trilogy, Sun, even a Belgian department store and a public museum are among those creating intense amounts of P2P value. By setting new standards, or through plain old 99 percent perspiration on the basics.

Their successes or practices, however, should not be your most important takeaways. Don't look for initiatives, programs, or technologies. Let's, instead, go back to the critical question raised earlier in this chapter: "Am I changing enough to demonstrate that I respect and trust the people around me?"

In a Work 2.0 world, your personal values — trust and respect in others, providing the freedom to act, and more — will be tested in completely new ways.

You already fund training and development. You approve IT budgets. You champion or manage process changes, infrastructure build-outs, and worktool designs. These are, indeed, all enablers for getting work done.

But Work 2.0 wants more from you. Are you willing to design budgets and strategies around what the people doing the work find most valuable? (Remember, more often than not, when it comes to collaboration, teamwork, learning, and communities, they're ahead of you.) Are you a peer-to-peer value revolutionary?

The future of great places to work will examine how much value you deliver when peers connect with peers.

4
Work 2.0 Is Extreme Leadership

06:30. Hit the deckplates. Within hours of meeting Rob Newson, I was whipping across San Diego Bay at 47 knots an hour, being subjected to tremendous forces as we made instant 180° turns, hurtling across the crests of our own waves.

Lieutenant Commander Rob Newson is a U.S. Navy SEAL, and XO (Executive Officer) of Special Boat Unit 12 and SEAL Team Seven. We were in an 11-meter RIB — Rigid Inflatable Boat — that can be dropped by helicopter, plane, or ship within 100 miles of a target. Its mission: insertion and extraction of a squad of eight SEALS, Green Berets, or Special Ops personnel. Often the goal of the mission, as Newson described it, is to "blow things up."

Your resolve to reinvent leadership must be the same.

Most of today's leaders are detached from the causes and effects of their actions on their employees' working capital. Leaders are shielded from the consequences of their decisions on how people's time, knowledge, or skills get wasted. Most are not forced to hurtle across the waves of tools, structures, managers, or communication that are anything but user-centered.

This detachment is visible, and the talent you most want to keep won't tolerate it for long.

Defining extreme leadership. "The idea is based upon extreme sports," says Newson, "where the true leaders trust their lives to their own talents, their tools, and the talents and direction of the people who support them. But the risk-taking is *not* about how daring one can be. It's all about vulnerability at the work level. That's where the real daily risks occur — not at the marketplace, political, or strategic levels."

Newson, who coined the term "extreme leadership," was one of 19 officers selected for a special project. They were to envision the U.S. Navy of 2020, including how its leaders must lead.

Like you, all military organizations are being forced to deal with new kinds of global threats. Many of the new enemies are small, fast insurgents who don't fight by the same rules we know so well. And like you, the military must also fight a war for talent.

Newson's model for extreme leadership was based on his own experience. "In the SEALS, leaders go through everything with their team. There is no separate course for officers. You do everything they do, except you get yelled at more. The leader is part of the group. He's never above the fray. I think this is an important dimension of the future. Unlike 20th-century leadership, tomorrow's talent will not settle for anything less than leaders who

> Shame on us if we're not ready to fight for talent according to the new rules

address the challenges faced by the people on the front lines."

He and his teammates designed the format for a 2001 Leadership Summit. The Navy committed to begin developing new views of leadership and driving them out to more than 600,000 personnel. Says Newson, "I mapped out all the ideas we wanted to cover: covenant leadership, empowered and empowering, trusted and trusting, teacher and learner, roving leadership, and lots more. But when it came time to name this multidimensional leadership, all the ideas we had sounded like a top-down perspective. They reinforced a separation between leader and everyone else. 'Extreme Leadership' popped into my head and it stuck."

The future of leadership is extreme accountability for life's precious assets. Tomorrow's leaders will shift from heroic management of people's time, attention, and talents to authentic respect for the assets the workforce brings with them.

Launching the new model. Jane Harper is experiencing this new accountability firsthand. She heads IBM's Extreme Blue, an 11-week summer internship for 100 computer-science and MBA students, worldwide.

The students are selected from the best of the best. One MBA student sits on each internship team, paired with three or four technical students. Some of the teams even have top-notch high schoolers working alongside the interns. They'll have the opportunity to join Extreme Blue upon entering college. Currently, the program is housed at IBM sites in Texas, Massachusetts, and Silicon Valley. Affiliated projects are also beginning in Germany, Israel, the UK, and Switzerland.

The students have regular access to the top ten leaders in the company, including CEO Lou Gerstner. They are mentored by some of the company's best technical and managerial minds. The projects they are assigned have tight three-month goals, and are sponsored by business units expecting breakthrough results. Spending $6 billion annually in research and development, IBM sees Extreme Blue as an academic incubator — cultivating the talent needed to create innovations.

"We started this program," says Harper, "because there was a breed of very talented folks out there that didn't consider IBM when leaving school. To change that, we've worked hard to create the ultimate internship experience.

"Before I was part of Extreme Blue, I thought I was in tune with the expectations people have of leaders and the companies they work for. Now, it's like, 'What was I thinking?' This experience has totally changed my view of what it will take to lead in tomorrow's environments. It now tracks with the themes of the new contract.

"First, there is no fear about pushing upward. These students know they've only got a couple months to deliver results, and they don't want their time or talent wasted." Role-playing a student's perspective, Harper reels off some of their criteria:

- "If I'm not working on something that is incredibly challenging and incredibly important, I'm not gonna be there." Harper says this is most important to her new hires, ahead any other criteria by a factor of five.
- "My Work My Way includes the way we need to work in order to meet the team's goals. Nonnegotiable are the best tools, total flexibility about how to achieve results, and completely open information-sharing."
- "Peer-to-peer value includes no loser managers." These students have complete confidence in themselves, she reports. And they want to be sure IBM doesn't hold them back.

"Before this sounds like too much me-me-me," Harper stresses, "it's important to emphasize that their criteria are based upon the expectations we laid out for them."

Each project team was given rigorous goals at the beginning of the summer. Projects included, among others, advances in Linux applications and wireless technology. Before returning to school, all the teams presented their results to an audience of 250 people at corporate headquarters, including CEO Gerstner;

president Sam Palmisano; the head of Technology, Nick Donofrio; and the head of HR, Randy McDonald.

Each team had only four minutes to explain the technical advances and business results expected from their projects. They then went into a Demo Conference, where they had to answer questions like How did you do this? What were you thinking when you did it this way? What are our competitors, Oracle and Sun, doing to beat this?

The final force of creative destruction. Harper observes: "I now really believe every rule in the book of leadership is changing. From a people perspective, we — as a company, as executives, as HR leaders — no longer set the rules. The talent everyone is going to fight over is now telling us: 'This is what we need in order to deliver the results you expect. This is what we'll accept. Otherwise we're not coming.'

"As leaders, shame on us if we're not ready to fight for talent according to the new rules," she concludes.

The future of leadership is extreme:

- You will have to understand risk-taking and work from a frontline perspective
- Your directives will be questioned in ways you've never experienced — all in the name of better work performance
- You will have to build trust and communication, tools and systems from the workforce's perspective
- Your integrity will be questioned if you pair "loser managers" with people who are passionate about doing their best

In short, you will have to shift from managing how people get work done to understanding how they do it. Then, you'll have to get ahead of those you're supposed to lead.

It's important to note that although Jane Harper learned these lessons from interns, extreme leadership isn't about kids dictating terms to seasoned senior execs. Grown-ups are a good thing! If the recent past has taught leaders anything, it's that maturity, wisdom, and profits are very important.

You should, however, pay close attention to the *honesty* of youth. They're willing to risk more early in their career by speaking the truth to power.

Respect that. Seek out the truth-tellers.

You need to surround yourself with people who will put their political ass on the line in order to reinvent peer-to-peer value, push for My-Way tools, and risk fighting the war for talent in completely new ways.

If you are going to be an extreme leader, your team will be composed of people who will make sure you deal with work-level barriers and concerns.

Four Forces of Creative Destruction

Call it enlightened self-interest: focusing on productivity by taking respect for the individual to completely new levels.

1. Work 2.0 is an Asset Revolution. Workforce assets include their time, attention, ideas, skills, knowledge, passion, energy, social networks, and more. How will you create better ROIs on these assets?

2. Work 2.0 is My Work My Way. The future of work is personalized and tailored. Information flows, tools, and compensation structures will be personalized so that people can have more control over their own destiny.

3. Work 2.0 is Peer-to-Peer Value. Nobody needs companies to help them collaborate, share, understand, or create. People can self-organize and connect amazingly well, thank you. You're a middleman. What value do you add when peers connect?

4. Work 2.0 is Extreme Leadership. The future of leadership is extreme accountability for life's precious assets. From this point forward, R-E-S-P-E-C-T includes better use of the assets the workforce brings with them.

chapter **3**

Workforce

What this means to you

[
It was the best of times.
It was the worst of times.
Charles Dickens

The first duty of a revolutionary
is to get away with it.
Abbie Hoffman
]

54

*T*he new contract will create a new age of wisdom for you and for all of us. And it will continue to be the age of foolishness. Work 2.0 will be the epoch of belief and the epoch of incredulity. We'll have everything before us; we'll have nothing before us.

Dickens was never so relevant.

A Meritocracy Is Both Intoxicating and Full of Tough Love

Yes, as more companies move into a Work 2.0 world, you and everyone around you will feel liberated. The new contract is about each person having more control over his or her own destiny. Whadda rush! That's what all of us want.

But, as your parents warned, you need to be careful what you wish for. You just might get it.

With greater freedom comes greater responsibility. In a Work 2.0 world, you'll need to be acutely aware of how your time, attention, ideas, knowledge, passion, energy, and social networks get used. Having more control over your own destiny also means increased accountability for linking your efforts to what really matters. It will be a lot harder to point outside of your team and say, "If only *they* did things differently."

WIIFM?
(What's in it for me?)

This book has been designed to help leaders think about difficult questions they are now facing. Undoubtedly, if they start lining up behind the new contact, you too will be facing tough questions. Like...

Am I ready to compete with the best of the best?

By definition, 80 percent of us cannot be in the top quintile of performers. "Workers with good ideas, or the ability to generate ideas, can write their own ticket. We're talking about the democratization of power," says Nathan Myhrvold, cofounder of Intellectual Ventures.[1] The new contract is a deeper democratization of power than we've seen to date. That also means fewer corporate safeguards protecting those who are not among the best of the best.

Am I ready to be 100% accountable for all my decisions?

You can run, but you can't hide. Work 2.0 will see to that.

What are my skills?

In a Work 2.0 world, personal branding, marketing, and networking will continue to increase. You've got to know your best skills and be able to market them. Big on the list of must-have skills: ability to research, synthesize, organize, recognize patterns in disparate events and information, facilitate, build scenarios, listen carefully, communicate simply and effectively, and learn quickly in almost any situation.

What are my weaknesses?

Think of this as the Wile E. Coyote Syndrome. In this brave new world, communication and accountabilities are transparent, and if you're in charge of what goes into My Work My Way, both your strengths *and* weaknesses will be exquisitely bared for all to see.

How long do I invest my assets in a company before I can expect a return?

This is one tough question. Many of us believe if we just hang in there just a l-i-t-t-l-e bit longer, our time or effort or the social connections we made will all pay off. In a Work 2.0 world, you'll need to make tougher decisions about when to stay and when to bail, with greater precision and speed.

How diverse-savvy am I, really?

Oh, sure, you respect people of all lifestyles, colors, and shoe sizes. But in the next decade, as globalization continues to disrupt your world, you will be teamed with people whose views about their working capital are very different from yours. The social aspects of globalization and diversity — while exciting — are still in their infancy, still simplistic. If Work 2.0 ramps up what leaders must do to demonstrate respect and trust, it will do the same for you. This could be one of the biggest challenges you will face as you connect with others.

What is my vision for my worklife?

Now, more than ever before, every day is a blank canvas. Work is becoming a portfolio of experiences that can be taken with you most anywhere. Do you *really* know what you want to be when you grow up? Your vision for yourself must guide more and more of your decisions. Because Work 2.0 won't eliminate crummy jobs, office politics, lousy bosses, or great opportunities that aren't really best for you. The new contract can't take care of all the information and choices that are thrown at you. You'll need a clear inner voice to guide you.

So your WIIFM is a much richer preparation for your role in a Work 2.0 world than you would get anywhere else. Use this book as a tool for envisioning new ways to articulate the assets you bring to any company, demanding the tools and support you need, and helping your team collaborate more effectively. (See Getting Started, page 61, for specific action steps.)

Why This Is a Leadership/Management Book

If this book helps you think about, and ultimately answer, questions like those above, then why wasn't it written as a simple self-help tool for the masses? Like: *How to Move Your Cheese in a Work 2.0 World.*

Your ability to change is critical to the successful jump to Work 2.0. But leaders must also set new standards for building and maintaining your work environment. In this book, I have set out to let leaders know what simpler, more productive, and great workplaces look like *from your perspective.*

Workforce: Jumping the Chasm

Work 1.0	Work 2.0
Social contract broken by "them"	Work contract developed by you, the talent
Getting permission, selling up	Driven by passion, or getting out
Maintaining energy, alignment	Walking away from energy bandits
Finding/making time	Walking away from timebandits
Respect, Trust, Integrity 1.0: How you are treated	Respect, Trust, Integrity 2.0: How you *and* your assets are treated
Holy Grail: Great place to work	Holy Grail: Great return on your investments

An example…

Any road warrior or vacationing family knows that, long before the September 2001 economic crisis, air travel had serious problems. During 1999–2000, crowded planes, gazillions of cancellations and delays, and oh-so-helpful communication from the airlines had made flying a happy-happy joy-joy experience. U.S. government representatives got tired of hearing passenger complaints. In their infinite wisdom, they passed a Passenger Bill of Rights, supposedly getting us all the respect we need. Yeah, right. Like mandating airline civility and courtesy is gonna help.

While better communication about flight delays certainly demonstrated a little more respect, it got nowhere near the root causes of passenger complaints. To create a breakthrough Passenger Bill of Rights, we needed to address:

- Airport security (which is finally a priority)
- The technology infrastructure that controls all air traffic
- The overscheduling of flights when everybody knows those planes won't take off
- The size of airports

A tricky balancing act occurs in an airport, where the problems are co-owned by so many different constituencies. That's not the case in most companies. Your leaders are solely accountable for your "air traffic control": the goals and infrastructure that drive your operations. They build the control tower. They allocate resources and set the standards for how you and your peers communicate and learn from each other. They determine the size and governance of your business units.

From *Simplicity:* Great companies execute. But simpler companies do one thing differently. They work backwards from what people need. They know that people will trust the corporate infrastructure to help them work smarter if the tools, processes, and information are grounded in their needs.

Hopefully, together, we can help your leaders work backwards from what you need to do great work.

What You Can Do:
Asset Revolutionaries Change What We Talk About

Be a provocateur. A pain in the butt. An advocate for personal productivity. An asset revolutionary. Question, question, question.

For you, the most important outcome from this book may be asking completely new questions. Of your leaders. And of yourself and your teammates.

Questioning leaders. George Bernard Shaw once said, "The reasonable man adapts himself to the world; the unreasonable one persists in trying to adapt the world to himself. Therefore, all progress depends on the unreasonable man." Please don't wimp out. Don't read this book, then say, "If only my boss would read this!" Be unreasonable; question how tools are built, how you and your managers are trained, how teams are formed. All progress is depending on you.

New questions for yourself. "Tut, tut, child," said the Duchess in Alice's Wonderland. "Everything's got a moral if only you can find it." If your journey through these pages is successful, it may raise just as many questions as answers. But they'll be completely new questions, guiding you toward different ways of working. Wrestle with them quickly. Jane Harper, describing new standards for extreme leadership in Chapter 2, confessed, "What we're doing now will be commonplace within three years."

If a Work 2.0 world is exciting to you, jump now!

Getting Started:
First Steps for Workers

1. Circulate the new contract
Discuss the new contract on pages 13–20 with your teammates. Discover the parts that are most relevant to your situation and your company. Let those discoveries change your conversation. A different conversation is what got the poor president, mentioned in Chapter 2, fired. For an emailable version, go to www.work2.com

2. Ask your boss new questions
Use what you learn to ask your boss new questions. Like:
- **To the point:** "How do I know that you value my time?"
- **Back door:** "How do you represent my workneeds to your boss?"
- **Tough love:** "How much of your time is spent doing great work?"
(If it's not enough for your boss, your portion is even smaller.)

3. Do your corporate homework. Complete the Index
Go to page 77. You'll find an index that tracks your company's Work 2.0 effectiveness. Fill it out. Circulate the results. The index has been a whack upside the head for many organizations! Emailable version: Go to www.work2.com

4. Do your personal homework. Make a list
Draw a line down the middle of a piece of paper. On the left, list all the new, introspective questions inspired by reading this book. (Some suggestions are on pages 56–57.) On the right, brainstorm all the resources that might help you answer your new questions. Include:
- Mentors, teammates, coaches, family, friends
- Books, websites, information sources
- Communities of practice, affiliations, workshops
Most people find they just created their first steps!

5. Speak the truth to those in power
Always.

section

2.

If You're Serious...

New Rules.

New Guiding Principles.

New Talent Wars.

Tools and tips to help you thrive
in a Work 2.0 world

Rule 1.
Embrace the Asset Revolution

Rule 2.
Build My Work My Way

Rule 3.
Deliver Peer-to-Peer Value

Rule 4.
Develop Extreme Leaders

chapter 4

Rule 1.

Embrace the Asset Revolution

Some people see things that are
and ask, Why?
Some people dream of things that never were
and ask, Why not?
Some people have to go to work
and don't have time for all that...

George Carlin

Great workplaces respect life's precious assets

According to the U.S. Bureau of Labor Statistics, overtime pay in manufacturing, including mandatory overtime, is near all-time highs. Many companies find it cheaper to buy more of a worker's life than to train another new hire. America Online (AOL) likes not paying at all. According to a *Forbes ASAP* 2001 audit: For ten years, AOL has used as many as 16,000 volunteers annually to host chatrooms and monitor online postings. Payment? Free AOL usage — currently $19.95/month. *Forbes* calculated that volunteer workers saved the company almost $1 billion in expenses between 1992 and 2000.

These strategies may work for good do-bies and some hourly wage earners, but most of your key talent want better returns on their time, knowledge, and social assets.

Smart companies will begin to fight the war for talent with an amazingly simple idea: improve business results and create a great place to work by improving how they use employees' time and energy.

OBSERVATIONS FROM THE 2.0 CAFÉ

If you want to see the front lines of the Asset Revolution, you might stroll through Colruyt, a chain of 150 discount stores in Belgium, which claims the lowest prices in the country.

Dirk Mortelmans and Johan D'Haeseleer are helping this retailer redefine how it uses working capital. Their business cards read "Werkvereenvoudiger" and "Simplificateur de Travail," Dutch and French for "Work Simplifier." Says Mortelmans, chief simplifier, "Our role is to save time and reduce hassles for employees and customers."

D'Haeseleer continues, "There are eight parts of our job":

1. Studying how real work gets done. Constantly observing the challenges employees face

2. Walking the floor — networking. Simplifying by walking around.

3. Being curious, asking lots of questions.
   [His actual words were, "Being a curious pain in the ass. Asking 'Why?' at least five times in each situation."]

4. Facilitating the conversations and planning that lead to simplification. "The discussions connect our culture and values to daily activities."

5. Focusing everything on productivity. "Hours should go down. Every second counts. Here, small is very beautiful. We'd rather have ten projects, which account for $1,000 each, than one for $10,000. And we measure the impact of each effort."

6. Teaching courses in work simplification — how and why it works at Colruyt.

7. Being lazy! "Being lazy is not the same as not being willing to work. It's one of the best ways to keep things very simple."

8. Focusing on lower prices for our customers and better profits for our firm.

D'Haeseleer reports that the work simplifiers have very specific targets. This year, they are productivity increases of 3 percent, reducing turnover by 150 people, and increasing the number of innovative ideas that get implemented by 50 percent.

The turnover/retention number is important to note. In a low-margin, high turnover industry, Colruyt is reinventing the war for talent by focusing on the work itself. Saving people time and hassles is key to where the new battles will be fought.

Employees everywhere — from discount stores to high-end knowledge workers — are seeking the same thing: Make it easier to do great work.

The Asset Trilogy

Within Colruyt's approach are three recurring disciplines that will run through any organization's effort to embrace the Asset Revolution:

- Observe, Measure, Discuss

The simplifiers walk the floor, observing how work gets done; measuring cost-savings and tracking pain-in-the-ass problems; and coaching through facilitated discussions. Tackle each of these disciplines, and you're on your way to creating a Work 2.0 environment.

Observe What Matters

Several years ago, Xerox couldn't figure out why its customer service reps were so inefficient. At call center workstations, the reps didn't follow the scripts they'd been trained to use. They kept jumping from one screen to another. Videotapes of their customer calls showed that (a) the scripted flow didn't correspond with how most customers asked their questions, and (b) the screen refresh rate was so slow that, in order to answer customer questions, the reps had to work around the so-called "efficient" process.

Xerox is hardly alone in being clueless about the way work really works. With all candor, most companies stink at observing how real work gets done and at recognizing what matters to the people doing that work. It's time to get disciplined about this. This lack of disciplined follow-through causes all sorts of wasted time and energy in organizations. If you want to improve how working capital gets spent, observe more!

Observation techniques can vary widely. Colruyt uses the observe-by-walking-around approach. By 2003, they will have 20 trained work simplifiers who roam stores and warehouses four days a week. Other firms, like Steelcase Furniture, use data-collection methods straight out of the social sciences of ethnography and anthropology. For example, seeking to understand how over 400 Oxygen Media employees performed in their New York offices, Steelcase videotaped them at work, had them fill out surveys, and even mapped their social networks with a proprietary software program.

"We're at the edge of a new era in work design, transforming the ways in which people work," says Joyce Bromberg, head of Steelcase's Environments and Advanced Application Design. "We actually codesign: The employees in client companies cocreate most everything. It's important to them that when their tools, infrastructure, and space all come together, hard work and soft, human, needs are fully integrated. One group of employees may need new collaborative space while another may need more control over information flow. Each solution will be unique. But every solution must start in the same way: observing how people work.

"As the design of work grows more disciplined, the transformation is going to force senior execs to make a critical decision," she says. "Are they going to focus on efficiency or effectiveness? Focusing on organizational efficiencies is much easier for a senior executive. Rarely does this approach include observing people at work, or serious consideration of social, intellectual, and human capital. Effectiveness is about getting the work done *and* thinking about how the work itself attracts and motivates people."

Indeed. Said more bluntly efficiency is a measure of how *you* believe time, talent, energy, knowledge, and social networks should be spent. Effectiveness tracks how the owners of those assets believe they should be spent. Both views are valid and important. As part of the war for talent, the workforce will be watching how you manage the tension between the two. Or whether you even try.

Measure What Matters

"What I love about my job is that it does have a very strong analytic component," says Ann Bamesberger, director of the Workplace Effectiveness Group for Sun Microsystems. Her background in civil engineering and her Stanford MBA are perfectly suited for engineering-driven Sun. Reflecting on her ten years there, she laughs: "I love being the crazy person within a sea of results, and among driven, intelligent, linear thinkers.

"Our mission is to design the work environment of the future," she says. "More and more, I'm discovering that the most important element is social. How we connect with each other as human beings is so critical. And it's the most difficult to track effectively. IT, which could be the biggest enabler in connecting people, is often the biggest barrier. So, we're trying to reverse-engineer optimal work environments — it's very important to work backwards from what people need to accomplish, and track how they get it all done.

"We've begun to build an entire metrics architecture around people's needs. Every six months we survey up to 6,000 employees worldwide, using standard pre- and post-intervention measures. What we track is personal productivity, whether employees can find the people they need to get their work done, how well teaming and collaboration needs are met, whether they can do quiet work when solitude and focus are necessary, and more."

As its first step toward this goal, Sun pioneered what they call a Network of Places. The idea is for employees to have access to the people and resources they need wherever they happen to be.

Their main work campuses are considered "hubs" of activity. Then "drop-in" spaces are built between campuses and employees' homes. Finally, all other workspaces — their homes, hotel rooms, or client offices — are considered linked "home ports." Bamesberger reports that purely through word of mouth, the first drop-in locations were full within two days of operation.

Sun describes their next step as launching an iWork strategy: following the model of the Internet and distributed computing. "We want people to have greater ability to work across space and time in the manner they choose," says Bamesberger. "The challenge isn't the technology. Much of what we need is available today. What's still missing is a next generation of management practices with which we can manage by results,

Early Examples

Colruyt	**Work Simplifiers:** Discount store dispatches real-time problem-solvers to work across processes and functions. Goal: Make it easier for people to make a difference; save them time
Oxygen Media	**Community-Based Planning:** With Steelcase, conducted deep study of workplace community norms and daily activities. Redesigned space according to how people really worked
Screaming Media	**The 21-Minute Meeting:** Company-wide disciplined approach to project meetings. Goals: Fast-track learning, review of accountabilities, waste no one's time. Results: Reduced status reports, increased project leaders' time to help each other
Sun Microsystems	**Drop-in Centers and iWork Strategy:** Began by using employee-commuting data, customer-needs data, and workneeds data to build mini-satellite offices. Moved on to build a measurement system focused on personal productivity

scale whatever we build, and still provide people greater control over how, when, and where they work. We're studying iWork carefully because we see a big opportunity to crack the code for a whole new way of managing."

Competitive pressure is forcing workplace measurement tools and systems, such as those developed at Sun and Steelcase, to become more commonplace. When you think about keeping up, do you know where to begin? What would you measure? How do you know what is really important?

The Jensen Group has been tracking six critical dimensions of New Economy workplaces since 1999. The short version of our tracking tool, the SimplerWork Index™, is on page 77. Fill it out! Share and compare the results. But be forewarned, you

New Faces You'll Need

The Fool	**Speaks the truth to power:** In medieval times, the Fool was the only one who could get away with it. Most execs need a confidant who will keep speaking the truth about how the company uses people's time and energy
New Quant Person	**Measures work design:** You will need someone who lives, breathes, and sleeps work-design data (see Steelcase and Sun stories)
New People Person	**"Gets" work design:** Sorry, most of HR is barren when it comes to solving people problems by focusing on the work itself. You will need someone who *thinks* people, but *sees* projects, systems, structures, tools

may not like what you learn. The head of Human Resources for a globally known company just compared his rankings with those of its employees — (their version of the tool was on a 1–10 scale, 1 being terrible, 10 being awesome):

- The head of HR gave his company 6s, 7s and 8s
- The employees gave the company 0s to 4s

It was quite an eye opener for this senior exec!

By the time I finished writing this book, more than 7,500 individuals in over 180 companies had taken the survey on page 77. Among the findings:

- Navigation: Companies are only 25 percent effective in helping employees find who or what they need to work smarter and faster
- Usability: Companies are only 15 percent effective in designing tools and processes focused on worker needs
- Time: Respect for individual's time was the lowest score — only 10 percent effective

Each of these findings demonstrates what's behind the new work contract. Employees are growing weary of firms that are clueless about workneeds.

Senior execs love the term "alignment," as in: "We all need to get aligned around our strategic plan." Well, if you want to win a Work 2.0 war for talent, you also need to measure and get aligned around the *employee's* view of what matters. In the future, great places to work will build deeper, more robust measurement systems around workneeds.

Discuss What Matters

Dialing back her passion does not appear to be one of Ann Bamesberger's core competencies. She continues: "Stop the madness! Let's quit building stupid, traditional environments. Stop it, stop it! Let's pay attention to what people need. I am paid to make smart decisions about our infrastructure. The truth is, I spend quite a bit of my time selling what our people tell us they need.

"There are three things most workers are seeking: more

freedom. More choices. And more control. People want more control over how their time gets used, and over anything that affects their future. More freedom to use what they know to make the right choices. And that freedom is based on having the right tools, support, and training to make those choices. Sun and all our competitors were beginning to make real progress up through mid-2000, looking at the questions, What do employees need that can we provide? What kind of freedom? What kind of choices? How much control? Then, six months later, because of economic pressures, it all came to a screeching halt. Well, guess what: Those workneeds didn't go away! They just went underground."

"Underground." A good term for where you'll find the Asset Revolution in most companies.

Do not be lulled into believing that a less-than-go-go economy has beaten back people's basic needs. If anything, when it gets harder to job-hop at will, the way people's time gets used becomes *more* important. So, too, their expectations for daily/weekly/monthly returns on their investments in your company. If these expectations and needs are not in your face, look underground.

The *most important action* you could take after reading this book will be to conduct a new kind of dialogue with your employees. Bring the underground discussion out into the open! After completing and sharing the SimplerWork Index, this might mean:

- Changing your 360° feedback process to include measuring management's effectiveness in helping people work smarter and faster
- Changing how you evaluate the effectiveness of communication and knowledge management
- Holding small group meetings with employees and asking them to rate the effectiveness of their tools and training
- Asking, in your next all-hands meeting, "How respectful are we of your time and attention, and are we focused on using it wisely and effectively?"

You already know that communicating with and engaging your employees is one of your most critical roles as a leader.

If you do nothing else, please use your leadership position to change the kinds of conversations that happen in your organization. Spread a powerful and simple idea: Any culture based upon respect for the individual must set new standards for respecting life's precious assets — your employees' time and energy.

Sponsor, sanction, and protect that conversation. Your employees will guide you thereafter.

Raising the Bar on Respect

For about two decades, the concepts of "worklife" and "balance" have been co-opted by well-intentioned people who design programs and initiatives. These programs — from daycare and eldercare, to concierge desks, vacations, sabbaticals, and more — mostly deal with life *outside* of work.

Work 2.0 employees certainly care about and appreciate these programs. But they'll seek more. They'll push further. You've got to deal with the work itself: how rewarding it is, how much learning is compressed into each day, how effectively a person's talents are used, and more.

Work 2.0 employees know that, of all the numbers that matter to you and them, one is immutable: 1440. That's the number of minutes in a day. Whatever percentage of those minutes they spend with your company, they want more out of what they invest, with less waste.

Compare your score to the Index score results, page 78

Getting Started Tips, page 79

SimplerWork Index™

Emailable version: Go to www.work2.com

Tracking the connections between great places to work
and what it takes to do great work

Six Great-Place-to-Work Dimensions for the New Economy

	STRONGLY AGREE	AGREE	NEITHER AGREE / DISAGREE	DISAGREE	STRONGLY DISAGREE
1. Competing on Clarity My manager organizes and shares information in ways that help me work smarter and faster	O	O	O	O	O
2. Navigation In my workplace, it is easy for me to find whomever or whatever I need to work smart enough, fast enough	O	O	O	O	O
3. Fulfillment of Basics In my workplace, it is easy to get what I need to get my work done — right information, right way, in the right amount	O	O	O	O	O
4. Usability In my workplace, corporate-built stuff* is easy to use (*Tools, training, instructions, information technology, etc.; all that is designed to help you do your work)	O	O	O	O	O
5. Speed In my workplace, that same corporate-built stuff gets me what I need, as fast as I need it	O	O	O	O	O
6. Time My company is respectful of my time and attention, and is focused on using it wisely and effectively	O	O	O	O	O

Short Version: Full questionnaire can be up to 50 questions

By the Numbers

SimplerWork Index: Year-end 2001: over 7,500 individuals, 180 companies

Competing on Clarity

Evaluates manager's effectiveness in helping individual work smarter and faster

45% Favorable

Navigation

Evaluates company's effectiveness in helping individual find who or what he/she needs

25% Favorable

Fulfillment of Basics

Evaluates company's effectiveness in work-oriented communication and

knowledge management

25% Favorable

Usability

Evaluates company's effectiveness in all that it designs to help people get tasks done

15% Favorable

Speed

Evaluates company's effectiveness in enabling employees to work in a 24/7,

ever-faster world

12% Favorable

Time

Evaluates company's respect for employees' time as an asset to be invested

10% Favorable

Statistics on website may differ. 7,500 people participated in controlled data-collection, which is

not on the website. Participation at the site is self-selected, under uncontrolled conditions.

Getting Started Checklist

Do	Don't
1. Observe what matters Watch how people spend time, talent, and energy doing real work.	**Plan employee asset allocations from the executive suite**
2. Measure what matters Track the difference between what you build and what people need. (See SimplerWork Index)	**Confuse employee satisfaction with workneeds satisfaction**
3. Discuss what matters Sponsor, sanction, and protect the dialogue that will propel you into a Work 2.0 world	**Bury the conversation, believing that makes it a nonissue**

chapter 5

Rule 2.

Build My Work My Way

Form follows function.

Louis Henri Sullivan, 1896

Afterwards, the universe will explode
for your pleasure.

Douglas Adams, a lifelong hitchhiker

Great workplaces get better results by giving people better control over their own destiny

Both swings of the pendulum in recent years have missed the mark. Dot-com me-ism gave employees stock options, foosball, and quality of life, but failed to deliver enhanced productivity or profits to their companies. For many, it represented the ultimate in self-indulgence. Post-crash corporate me-ism — slashing budgets and people — is equally bankrupt: It provides short-term relief but few sustainable solutions, and breeds fear and cynicism among those who are left to do the work.

My Work My Way sits between those two overreactions. It customizes information, worktools, and experiences to individual needs, but it is specifically targeted to enhance business success, productivity, and personal effectiveness.

For individuals. Work is getting so complicated, interconnected, and fast that it's fully appropriate for employees to seek My-Way customized experiences in each and every one of your tools and systems. It's the only way they'll be able to keep up with the pace of change, do their best, and manage their lives as well as their work. But My-Way customization also puts your employees on the hook for greater accountabilities. By definition, as work becomes more and more customized, every employee assumes greater ownership and more responsibility for results.

For companies. By focusing on increased personal productivity and effectiveness, companies get faster bottom-line results at cheaper cost because frontline and mid-level employees can figure out what they're supposed to do much faster. That's the great news. Now for the challenge: Are you willing to change your relationship with your employees? My Work My Way advances will change how they make personal choices. Are you willing to win by giving people better control over their own destiny?

OBSERVATIONS FROM THE 2.0 CAFÉ

Where to begin: If your My-Way efforts include tailored compensation plans, you'd be on target. Same with creating customized information tools, portals, and knowledge management. Personalized training and development plans? Yup. Tailored eLearning, flextime, vacations, sabbaticals, virtual work agreements, and more: yes, yes, and yes.

Trying to analyze all the My-Way tactics and tools and pick the best place to start could make your head explode. Too, too much! So don't.

Instead, focus on how My Work My Way will change your relationship with your employees. Giving people greater control over their own destiny demonstrates a deep respect for individuals that is sorely lacking in many companies.

Consider the power of one-to-one relationships with *customers*. If your organization is truly committed to customized customer experiences (not just packaging your cost-cutting efforts under the banner of customer focus), you know the impact that customization can have. Your customers keep coming back because you eliminate hassles, anticipate their needs, and make it easier for them to be their best.

Same with your best employees. The emergence of My-Way tools and cultures raises the standard for what it means to be a great place to work. The workforce isn't interested in a free ride. Just an environment that customizes work, making it easier for them to do their best.

So a My-Way culture sets new corporate accountabilities for: Know me. Know my work. Know what motivates me. Know what I need. Know how to help me. (See sidebar on page 86, itemizing the nine dimensions of My Work My Way.)

At the same time, it increases the degree to which employees feel ownership of their objectives, personal development, and outcomes. Once an employee assumes greater accountability for his or her personal productivity — by designing a personalized learning plan, organizing how corporate information is structured, or participating in the selection of teammates — there's no turning back. It's no longer some senior exec insisting that employees own the next big challenge. They are active co-owners.

The Doctor Is In

Dr. Michael Rich may be seem like an unusual choice to illustrate the business benefits of My Work My Way. Yet he understands the power of observing how work gets done, how tools change relationships, where to limit freedom and choices and where to expand them...and more.

Rich is a 47-year-old Harvard-educated physician specializing in adolescent medicine at Children's Hospital in Boston. He's in an academic group practice, so he has added responsibilities for training medical students and residents.

Prior to his medical studies, he spent 12 years in the film industry. Mostly directing documentaries. A personal high was a two-year stint in Japan, assisting famed director Akira Kurosawa.

Combining his two careers, Rich gives his patients video cameras. They use video to document and teach him about their work of getting better — how they take their meds, what they do to keep life-threatening diseases under control, the stress they're under, and more. In turn, he more effectively teaches them how to take greater accountability for the challenges they face.

Rich is modeling the use of a My Information, My

Productivity tool. The fact that it's a video camera isn't important. What is important is the shift in the doctor-patient (read: manager-employee) relationship. The patient has greater control over and contributes more to their exchanges. Result: Everyone involved learns and changes faster.

Old Way vs. 2.0 My-Way
WHAT'S THE DIFFERENCE?

The Old Way focuses on creating a great place to work with golden handcuffs: making it hard for other firms to duplicate your perks, benefits, and culture — with little emphasis on productivity or ramping up personal accountability. Great approach...if you can afford it.

Old Way Model: Employees click their heels three times before crossing your threshold: "There's no place like work, there's no place like work..."

Old Way Poster Child, BMC Software: Bank, store, dry cleaner, hairdresser, nail salon are all on campus. Same with gym, basketball court, horseshoe pits, beach volleyball. Cooks select the day's greens from onsite garden. Employees have spaces for naps and taking sculpture classes.

2.0 My-Way Poster Child: None yet. But isolated practices are popping up all over. Consider these shifts toward My Compensation: While laying off almost 10 percent of its workforce, Charles Schwab included in its severance packages a $7,500 "hire-back" bonus for any employee rehired within 18 months. And rather than go into full layoffs, Accenture offered partially paid sabbaticals of up to 12 months for about 1,000 employees. Firms are customizing more in order to reduce costs and still retain more of the people they have already recruited, trained, and developed.

The 2.0 Model, and Toughest Challenge: The winners in the new war for talent will be the firms who take a holistic view across all nine My-Way dimensions, and tailor their approach to best satisfy customers, employees, and shareholders.

The essence of his approach is that sustainable success occurs only when people are in control of their own destiny. This is at the heart of My Work My Way, and his comments provide a map of the values and leadership qualities your employees are seeking. If you replace "patient" with "employee," and see the parallels between medical and business challenges, the guideposts you need are here.

Dr. Rich on the power of My-Way tools: "I use video cameras less because of my background in film than because, on my own, I see so little. Most of what my patients do to get better is invisible to me, beyond what I experience when I am with them. The camera is a bridge between my medical work of diagnosing and managing, and my patients' very human work of change.

"At first, the videotapes helped me see what I needed to know to help patients manage their disease. It was incredibly helpful to see the mother of a child with asthma who was still smoking in the house, when she swore to me that she had stopped. But far more valuable insights from the tapes came in ways I never expected. Like how I approach a diagnosis. When I look at the world through my patients' eyes, I discover questions I never thought to ask.

"The way we [doctors] structure information, and the way we're taught to elicit information from a patient, completely miss the boat! All of our questions are framed from our own perspective on a situation. No matter how friendly the doc is and how caring he is as a coach, the doctor-patient relationship keeps control of information in our hands. That's wrong. Ultimately, the illness is the patient's problem.

"The power of using a patient's language — his or her ways of structuring ideas — to communicate is that it immediately allows the patient to take more ownership of the work of getting better.

"Ultimately, there's one big reason for changing the control of information. That's time. With managed care, I'm supposed to spend just 15 minutes with a patient. That's ridiculous! I care for teenagers — adolescents barely say 'hello' in the first 15 minutes. Giving them more control of the flow of ideas means I can get more accomplished for them in shorter periods of time."

On trust, respect, and statistical results: "When I hand a patient the camcorder, I say, 'I want you to teach me about your experience.' Every one of them has said that act takes our relationship to a new dimension. My trust for their view of

The Nine Dimensions of My Work My Way

Great benefits, vacations, programs to help family life, etc. — all the good stuff from Work 1.0 — are still meaningful to employees. Work 2.0 goes further. It's about making and keeping promises on the productivity basics: Know me. Know my work. Know what I need. Know how to help, and reward, me.

Description	Early Pioneers
1. **My Boot Camp** As numbers of free agents and instant-teams soar, orientation for new hires gets strategic	**Trilogy Software** places every new hire on a three-month fast track. Month 1: Mentoring begins and instruction tracks are assigned. Month 2: Projects are assigned. Month 3: Employees focus on finding their place in, and impact on, the entire organization
2. **My Compensation** Base, bonus, equity are selected cafeteria-style; More guarantees are being negotiated	**Trilogy** and other high tech-firms started to build the models with which employees create their own compensation packages. Many dropped or back-burnered this idea when the economy cooled. (Pressure's off. Yeah, right.)

what's going on in their world demonstrates completely new levels of respect.

"The camera changes how we communicate with each other. Patients say it gives them freedom to tell me about what they're facing. It helps them express their whole problem in ways that never come out when I frame the flow of information. So the child with asthma could tell me about her mother's smoking without blaming her. Or kids who don't want to express their stress or fear can let me know in a less direct fashion. The

---

3. **My Coach**
Personal coaches
become more common

At Corning, one scientist is assigned the role of "motivator" and another has the role of "bridge" — enhancing cross-functional work. They are held accountable for improving results

---

4. **My Future**
Simulation technology
will soon go
mainstream; low-tech
tools also grow

Over the next few years, as sim-tech becomes cheaper and more widespread, look for increased use of sophisticated personal planning tools for teaming, managing workflow, making life and career choices, and more

---

5. **My Information,**
My Productivity
There is unlimited
potential in tailoring
and customizing

Oh, the My-Way possibilities for intranets, portals, and all info-tech! So far, it's unfulfilled potential; hardly any are user-centered. Among the exceptions: **Landstar** wireless systems — truckers track available loads, save days in coordinating round-trips

---

6. **My Learning**
Deliver just-in-time,
practical,
useful, and
on-demand
solutions

eLearning solutions abound, but few are designed backward from the needs of the people doing the work. Among the exceptions: **Dell** assemblers get just-in-time learning focused on the tasks before them. **Microsoft, IBM,** and **Cisco** are collaborating on CLEO: Customized Learning Environment Online

---

camera gives them ways to record these ideas and show how their lives are affected.

"Also, the process is empowering. Every patient senses, and takes on, increased personal accountability. Their self-awareness increases. They learn faster. Right now, I'm preparing a paper [for a medical journal] in which we measure and demonstrate a change in patients' overall wellness. Simple self-examination, through the use of the camera, has created statistically significant improvements in their wellness and quality of life."

7. **My Space** Deliver customized workspaces for the multi-tasking worker	**Cisco** formed its Workplace Resources Unit to align how it responded to employee needs with corporate goals. Collaborative spaces, private spaces, and IT structures were redesigned. 34% of its workforce now makes regular use of mobile workplace options.
8. **My Team** Current team members select future teammates	**Southwest Airlines** established the standard for teammates (pilots, maintenance crew, everyone) to select new teammates. **Microsoft** enhanced the approach by adding rigorous testing for skill fit.
9. **My Tools** Supply my hardware, my way	**CSC United Kingdom** has experimented with outsourcing hardware purchases to its employees. They get a budget and compatibility criteria. It's then up to them to get the tools that best meet their needs.

Note: A tenth, unavoidable dimension of My-Way is also heading your way.

My Health Plan: easily transferable health benefits. It is left off this list only because it will require major governmental and regulatory changes. But it is guaranteed to hit if rising healthcare costs and free-agency trends continue unabated.

As the Work 2.0 model has emerged, some providers have begun to develop unique solutions to My-Way needs. One of the early pioneers is Towers Perrin, a leading human resource consulting firm. What they call mypay-myway and myjob-myway cover two of the nine dimensions.

On compliance and commitment: "In the medical profession, 'compliance' is a measure of how well a patient does in what she's supposed to do (like taking her meds on time, in the right doses). But to my ear, compliance is what a slave does for a master! Instead, I talk about 'adherence' because, to me, that means the patient and I came up with a plan together. If she can't adhere to it, the problem is not with the patient but with the plan. So we modify the plan. That's really important to her total commitment to whatever we do."

On ownership and accountability: "I have a remarkable success rate when it's crucial that patients make a commitment to change — like with stopping smoking, or with chronic problems like asthma — because I insist they own the problem. Once they own it, once they know there is no magic pill, they start making the hard decisions. In those cases, they do most of the work, not me. They control how most of the change happens and how we communicate about it. Much of my job is then listening and coaching."

On building people-oriented systems that work: "In the mid-twentieth century, in order to be more efficient in delivering medical care, we moved toward problem-oriented medicine. Doctors focus on specific illnesses and become experts in those areas. Efficiencies are good, but with that change we also made people the receptacle for problems.

"Over the years, I've discovered that a lot of the challenges we face in delivering medical care is that we don't see the whole person in front of us. We're not building systems and structures — from small (like video cameras) to big (like how we set up hospitals) — in ways that allow patients to bring their own strengths, experience, and wisdom to the table.

"This problem continues in my own hospital. We recently underwent a major management change and restructuring. Ernst and Young was brought in to evaluate how we could improve our operations. They asked me what improvements I would make in how the hospital was managed. I said, 'I have only one recommendation. I'd like each member of the new management team to spend one day in every clinic: Work shoulder to shoulder with us. See what we do. Understand our product, service, and our patients. And *then* design your structures, systems, and processes. Please don't plan the way you think it should work, then fit the docs and patients into the model. The abstract ideal is not responsive to the real.'"

Back in the Business World...

If you need a more direct business take on the ideas Dr. Rich has laid out, the following are excerpts from a conversation with Tom Kelly, vice president of Internet Learning Solutions for Cisco, whom we'll meet again in the next chapter.

Tom Kelly on My-Way tools: "We're currently piloting several Web-based tools: My Training, My Future, My Career. With these tools, an employee and her manager can track whether she's keeping up with the learning requirements of the job. Before they start, each employee reviews a list of what's important to her job, and checks off what she wants to learn more about. We set up for each employee a learning box that works much like an email box or voicemail box. Whenever an employee has a few minutes, she can open her learning box and view the modules that meet her learning needs and goals.

"We've divided the key learning opportunities and content

New Faces Redux

The previous chapter mentioned that you need a **new People Person** — one who "gets" work design — as well as a **new Quant Person**, who measures work design. The accountabilities within these roles are supercritical to your My-Way efforts. Without them, you *would* be building an entitlement cookie jar.

into small chunks. The modules average about 10 to 12 minutes; some are as short as five minutes. We're working hard to keep them small so that people can easily go through them and move on. We've also built My History so that each person can track his or her progress. It works like an email folder. Employees can save the unread modules, and file or delete the ones already viewed."

On alignment and communication: "At Cisco, our first priority — customer satisfaction — is followed closely by employee satisfaction. That means, as part of our My-Way efforts, we make sure everyone gets information on the company and priorities in ways that best meet their needs. Access to corporate messages, with no filtering, is really important. Employee communications from [CEO] John Chambers are video- or audio-taped and made available to every employee on the planet within 36 to 48 hours. So nobody has to worry about what John says being filtered through layers of translations, with various translations or personal bias."

On the challenges ahead of us: "We, like everyone else, are still focused on how to *teach* more effectively. The next frontier is to better understand how people *learn*. What everybody's doing right now looks like the way movies were made a hundred years ago — bringing the camera in front of a stage and filming a play. So far, Orson Wells hasn't shown up to show us how to use our tools to truly communicate and connect with people on an individual level. So the future is about greater understanding: how people learn, how to engage each person differently, and how to provide each person with a unique experience."

Getting Started Tips, page 92

How to know that your My-Way efforts are successful, page 93

Getting Started Checklist

It's the culture, stupid! The goal behind My Work My Way is to enhance productivity by giving your employees greater control over their own destiny. The care and feeding of the assets that each individual brings with him or her demonstrates deep respect, and circles back to benefit the company in the short and long term.

Do	Don't
1. Use your business model Know thyself. Which of the nine dimensions of My Work My Way would have the most impact on productivity and effectiveness?	**Start by copying other firms' "best practices" — unless you're copying their culture**
2. Start small and fast, win big Most firms will find the info-tech dimension, My Info, to be easiest and fastest — *if* you're ready to give up some control	**Start with the initiatives that ask the least change of your senior team**
3. Track what happens Understand the connections between My-Way changes and changes in bottom-line/top-line results	**Make My-Way a flavor of the month** Your employees will leave faster than ever

BUILDING MY WORK MY WAY

Tracking Your Success

THE FIVE QUESTIONS OF BEHAVIORAL CHANGE

When people make decisions to act, they seek the answers to these five questions.* If your My-Way efforts are successful, the majority of your employees should be able to answer these questions **without their manager.** For each new project or initiative, the tools, information, and processes you provide should help them **answer these questions on their own.**

- How is this project, or change, relevant to what I do?
- What are my next steps? (What, specifically, should I do?)
- What do success and failure look like?
- What tools and support are available?
- WIIFM — What's in it for me? For us?

*The Behavioral Communication Model — how it works and why — is fully detailed in *Simplicity*. Wording of questions has been adapted for use in *Work 2.0*.

chapter 6

Rule 3.

Deliver Peer-to-Peer Value

> Without deviation from the norm,
> progress is not possible.
> **Frank Zappa**

Great workplaces get more out of collaboration by putting more into it

First, let's all pay homage to the gods of Great Culture, Teamwork, and Shared Values. Now, permission to move on?

Good. Because, while these disciplines are supercritical, as currently practiced, they'll only get you to the ground floor in Work 2.0.

Managers are W-A-Y behind on how to add value to employee collaboration. Why? New standards are being daily set for what is valued in those exchanges. Like: What content is most valuable, and what social connections, timing, tips, and tools are needed; how to achieve the right balance between context setting and detail; and what type of coaching would be most helpful.

Who sets those standards? Employees do, when they're connecting with each other — without your involvement. Your centralized, top-down approach to planning simply isn't keeping up with the rate of new devices, new ways to connect, and new ways to share information. If you are going to add value to peer-to-peer exchanges, you must be willing to design budgets and strategies around what the people doing the work find most valuable. That means a lot more listening before you plan.

To get more from collaboration, you've got to put more into it: more understanding of how employees *want* to share with each other, and more attention to what they *need* to collaborate effectively.

OBSERVATIONS FROM THE 2.0 CAFÉ

Why worry about raising the standards for peer-to-peer collaboration? Let's face it, many companies — possibly yours — still need to master yesterday's standards. The ideas in this chapter will only add more challenges for you.... So, why bother?

The reason is simple. The overall talent pool — especially A-level talent — is shrinking into a talent puddle.

For a couple of decades now, statisticians have warned us of an upcoming blip in the demographic supply chain. Not new news. It's just reality now. A tough economy complicates the problem because you can't afford to hire the talent that is becoming available due to layoffs. All this means fewer people have to get more done.

How? Hypercollaboration: More people have to get more out of every collaborative exchange.

Sure, intense collaboration begins with selecting the right people, aligning their goals, and working under shared values. But that does not mean your P2P responsibilities have ended once you declare, "Here's the goal. Go forth and be empowered." Nor is it enough to "champion" or "sponsor" team efforts.

We live in the Attention Economy. As Tom Davenport and John Beck describe in their book of the same name: "Understanding and managing attention is now the single most important determinant of business success. If you want to be successful in the current economy, you've got to be good at getting attention."[1] The big-picture items (values, mission, goals, etc.) are no longer enough to focus your employees' attention.

The authors then describe your main P2P challenge: "Given all our experience with attention industries — [TV, movies, advertising, and others] — you would think we'd all be expert at applying their lessons to manage attention effectively in business. But we're not."[2]

If you want more people to get more out of collaboration, you've got to get better at respecting their time, earning their attention through user-centered and learner-centered design, and fueling their passions and imagination with what they find exciting.

That means you're on the hook for

- Just-in-time, on-demand learning that continually draws employees back for more
- Better, more useful content for collaboration
- Destroying the boundaries between play and work, between informal and formal learning
- Creating the space and time to think — sometimes slowing things down enough for all the lessons within peer-to-peer collaboration to sink in

All of this, and more, is what your employees find when they collaborate in the outside, networked world. It's what they find

Pop Quiz

Since games can spark people's imaginations, can you
match our Work 2.0 Café interviewees...

1. Tom Kelly, VP of Internet Learning Solutions, Cisco

2. Peg Maddocks, Senior Manager, Learning Tools and Solutions, Cisco

3. Karen Stephenson, President, NetForm International, helping companies study and leverage their social networks

...with their biographical factoids?

a. Personal goal: Iron Butt Rally, 11-day, 11,000-mile motorcycle ride

b. Hobby: Tending 80 bonsai trees. "I learn patience, how to pay attention to the smallest details, and how to make a difference by doing a little bit each week."

c. Ex-kindergarten teacher, with a Ph.D. in instructional psychology. "Everything I know about how people grow I learned in kindergarten."

d. Theater major in college. Wanted to be a world-famous movie director

e. Harvard-trained Ph.D. in anthropology. Great-grandfather hunted with Buffalo Bill Cody

f. Stared down the wrong end of a renegade soldier's rifle in war-torn Central America. Visit to Mayan ruins was cut short. Jeep was stolen

(Answers are on page 109.)

valuable in hurry-up-and-get-it-done-now environments, where their attention is pulled in infinite directions. If you are going to help employees jump into hypercollaboration, you are going to have to do more to create this type of value.

Pretty hard to accomplish if you had to do so in a traditional top-down fashion! Fortunately, you don't. You just need a good set of ears and eyes. If you're willing to let them, your employees will teach you what they need, and what they find most valuable.

Two Principles to Guide You

For all this talk of peer-to-peer value, let's come back to the obvious: The reason for better collaboration is better business results. To get there, keep two principles in mind:

- **For quickest results,
  live where customers and employees meet**
  You can deliver peer-to-peer value anywhere in the organization, but changing how you help those who are closest to the customer will offer the fastest short-term returns. You need to go beyond "The Customer Is King." Get in the trenches and learn about the real challenges employees face as they focus on the customer.
  Then deliver useful content and addictive learning. More simply: Supply great stuff to talk about, and great talk happens!

- **For true competitive advances,
  study the invisible workplace**
  The social networks inside your company make *everything* work. If you're serious about real competitive advances, get disciplined about understanding the invisible, social workplace. Study the social bonds between peers and how those connections influence the success (or failure) of every project. If this sounds too warm and fuzzy, think of it as due diligence. An awful lot of the available

working capital in your company is expended on peer-to-peer interaction. If you're going to cut costs *and* build a great place to work, you really need to know how social networks work.

Live Where Customers and Employees Meet

Tom Kelly thanks his mom for his outlook on life, and the way he takes on tough assignments. "She encouraged me to challenge authority in a positive and respectful way. So when people tell me 'That's impossible,' my response is, 'It's not impossible if I can do it.' I look for environments that encourage autonomy and creativity. That's what I love about my role at Cisco."

Kelly's primary responsibility is to provide product and technical training to Cisco's sales force and account managers, using eLearning solutions. He is also passionate about finding ways to get employees better returns on their working capital.

"There are two things everyone gives at work that they can't get back," he says. "Time and emotion. If people invest these things, they deserve the best return we can provide. They deserve more control over their own future." With a keen eye for human nature, Kelly notes that people also want to *talk about* their investments, how they control their own destiny while meeting customer needs, how they spend their time, what excites them, and what ticks them off. "So that's where we started," he says. "We listened to what our sales force was talking about."

Begin with the basics. Kelly credits his partner, Peg Maddocks, for delivering the first eLearning solutions that employees found truly valuable. "We started with customer-focused but mundane tasks," she says, "like how to do a purchase order. By capturing an expert's keystrokes and voice, we created over 300 mini-movies of application demonstrations, and delivered them over the Internet. Not very exciting, I'll admit. But for the first time, employees started trusting us for 'I-need-this-now-and-I-need-it-to-be-easy' solutions."

From there, Maddocks focused on Cisco's field sales team, chunking and organizing over 8,000 "information nuggets" culled from various white papers and presentations. She reports that prior to this step, "it felt like we were asking the people in the field to go to 8,000 places to learn how to do their job." The result was not only easier and more useful searches, but Cisco further refined the learning process by tying it to individual assessments.

To build these self-assessments, Maddocks did a full analysis of the sales process. For example, she studied the major steps an account manager has to complete to make a sale, and catalogued all the activities within each step. By doing this up-front work, Cisco built a user-centered system: customized so that all the people in the field get only what they need, exactly when and how they need it.

The Maddocks/Kelly team then deepened their efforts, focusing on the conversations between customers and the sales force. They created an Account Manager Learning Environment (AMLE).

Maddocks continues, "We found that our account managers were saying, 'I need to talk to CIOs, CEOs, and CFOs, but they

P2P Defined

How people are different from computers, and very much the same

According to www.openp2p.com, what makes P2P *computing* unique is that individual nodes operate with significant or total autonomy from central servers, and that ownership of computing resources is decentralized. Like it or not, your employees see collaboration with others **in the same way.** Their exchanges have significant autonomy from central servers (read: Corporate) and they own their working capital, not you. **What's different** is that the sharing of P2P value between people *can* involve computers, but doesn't have to.

usually care about different things. How do I talk to different types of people?' Since they wanted to be able to get their hands on this information just prior to talking with clients, each module within AMLE is organized like a series of conversations — providing different ways to answer client questions about technology, depending on whether they come from a CIO, CEO, or others.

"If, however, the account manager doesn't need the dialogue structure, he or she can go directly to a 'cheat sheet,' which is a database linked to all those information nuggets."

Going viral. "Our initial solutions were all about trust. Once account managers trusted us to help them with client conversations," Maddocks concludes, "they changed how they talked to each other. They started sharing more. They started using more AMLE content to drive their conversations." As an example, Maddocks points to the pilot of the AMLE system. Thirty account managers were asked to test it. Within weeks, 300 unique subscribers had signed up, on their own.

Tom Kelly provides another example: "We recently launched a learning module as an interactive game, similar to Jeopardy. The goal was for account managers to learn the fundamentals of a specific Cisco technology. We tested it with 300 account managers, 10 percent of the target audience, just to see what would happen. We didn't communicate it broadly, and there were no rewards for playing." Kelly notes, tongue in cheek, that it appealed to the competitive nature of salespeople: "'See if you can score higher than the high school kids who've played.'

"Within 60 days," he says, "3,000 people were playing and talking about the game. Every person that played it shared it. Everyone thought the module was valuable, useful, and so engaging that they had to share it with others. The module went viral and global — regions shared it with other regions. All of a sudden, people were intrigued by, and talked about, the basic information they needed to do their job."

Behind the curtain. Cisco's AMLE system illustrates some of the peer-to-peer basics that are necessary to jump into hypercollaboration.

First: Cisco began where customers and employees met. The company is earning trust in the trenches by delivering useful solutions — "useful" as defined by the people who do the work. Kelly and Maddocks asked, "What would make it easier for account managers to interact with customers and solve their problems?"

Next: AMLE focuses on real-time, on-demand solutions. Whatever you deliver to the front lines — content, learning, coaching, etc — must be ready for immediate application. It must have low to no learning curve and be immediately useful.

John Cone, VP of Learning for Dell Computer, calls this "stealth learning." Says Cone: "We talk about the micro-bite, a chunk of knowledge about five minutes long....Education within Dell is 'built to order' since this is the only way to ensure that education stays current with business needs."[3] Real-time solutions are not just about going faster. Give people precisely customized information, and they will have more time to collaborate. That's peer-to-peer value in a Work 2.0 world.

Finally: When Tom Kelly says that the recent learning modules went viral, he's referring to the ultimate peer-to-peer value: It's a rush to discover more! There's learning...and then there's LEARNING!, where the personal experience, or "aha," is so intense that people need to share it. Gaming and simulations are among the most talked about forms of corporate content between employees because it's exciting to share and compare personal mastery with others. (Including friendly competition. Says Kelly about their latest game: "I wouldn't be surprised if somebody lost a couple bucks on their scores.")

I'm sure you've noticed that I haven't spent a lot of time talking about extraordinary teamwork or community-building. Of course they're important. Critical, even. But here's a hidden rule for creating intense peer-to-peer value: Give people more real-time, exciting, useful, and addictive stuff to talk about.

Human nature will take over from there!

People love talking to people. And they're amazingly good at self-organizing and selecting what's good to talk about. (They'll do it anyway, without your assistance. Then, it's called a grapevine.) Pour more awesome stuff into their collaboration, and you'll get better results back. Pour in useless corporate logic and strategies, and...well, you get the idea.

No time to waste! In the time it takes to read this sentence, someone is raising the standards for now, wow, and addictive content and learning. Tom Kelly confirms that Cisco plans to be one of the standard-setters.

"We've begun conversations with top companies in simulation gaming — like Electronic Arts [the creators of the successful Sims family, Sim-City and Sim-Earth] and Blizzard Entertainment — about partnering with us. Imagine Sims as an office environment. Instead of a family situation, imagine a team of four or five people trying to make a sales call or get a project done. No one person would have control, and the players would have to collaborate in completely new ways to close the sale.

"In my don't-tell-me-it's-impossible mind," Kelly continues, "I can see us delivering learning modules as a simulation game that account managers would play ten minutes a day for 30 days. We could simulate an entire year on the job in that time. They'd be able to see whether they had made enough sales calls,

New Faces...Again

If you wish to create peer-to-peer value, the role of **new People Person** who "gets" work design is supercritical. Someone needs to be accountable for the place where infrastructure and people meet: keeping up with how employees are setting the new standards for collaboration.

And the accountability of social due diligence falls on the shoulders of the **new Quant Person,** who measures work design.

whether they made quota, how they did on customer
satisfaction, and whether they would remember to go home
and have a family life! Tools like this would deliver on the
new work contract — helping people see during their first
month on the job what the next year of their work will be like.
Nobody's done this yet, but if anyone does," concludes Kelly,
"I think it's going to be Cisco."

During the next few years, great places to work will create
addictive learning (where it's a rush to keep coming back for
more!) and exciting collaboration by creating stuff people
really want to talk about. Some, like Cisco, will rely heavily
on technology. Others, such as Trilogy Software, will increase
face-to-face brainstorming. In the next chapter, you'll learn
more about how this firm reinvented Trilogy University by
designing an entire semester of new-hire interaction around
customer needs.

Standardsetters like these, who create intense peer-to-peer
value, will blow today's Work 1.0 collaboration methods out
of the water.

The Invisible Social Life of Your Workplace

Fascinating blindspot: When companies want to know what
trend is around the corner, or how to position a product, they'll
think nothing of studying customer views to the nth degree —
tweezering lint from their customers' belly-buttons for clues
about what they'll buy. But truly study how social networks
make everything work inside that same company? "Hrrrmmph"
is the likely response. "Waste of energy." Few senior execs see
the value in this type of investment.

This blindspot becomes a managerial problem when we
examine how technology has increased the power behind face-
to-face encounters and social networks. The *Wall Street Journal*
pointed this out after the fall of the Twin Towers demonstrated
the global need to be together and share common experiences.
They noted that in the past five years, "email became
ubiquitous, but the yearning for physical handshakes

didn't abate."[4] Technology merely places on overdrive our social need to connect with each other. Which, in turn, radically changes the importance of the invisible social structures within your organization.

Karen Stephenson, president of NetForm, is one of the people who get the call when execs do "get it." NetForm maps the invisible workplace, identifying the go-to people within organizations based upon their social connections. Stephenson likens her role to a radiologist for organizations. "The key to how companies accomplish their goals," she says, "is in the relationships between employees."

Stephenson is passionate about the value of understanding social networks. One of her earliest clients was the Centers for Disease Control and Prevention in Atlanta, Georgia. In the late 1980s, she helped them track the social network of Gaetan Dugas, a French-Canadian flight attendant. Dugas became known as "Patient Zero" for his infamous and pivotal role in spreading the AIDS virus across North America.

Since then, NetForm has become a leader in helping companies improve business results by understanding the informal networks within their hierarchies. Among others, Stephenson has consulted with Merrill Lynch on its organizational structure and global effectiveness, helped U.S. Navy staffers break free of their need to "sell up the chain of command" before they could collaborate, and worked with the Los Angeles Police Department to change its community outreach effort in light of the Rodney King beating.

How your invisible workplace is structured. The currency may be body fluids, justice, or information exchanges, but Stephenson insists all patterns of social behavior are very similar. "We have done more than 300 in-depth corporate studies," she says. "We've discovered a powerful set of rules that allow us to recommend changes with predictable outcomes. Insisting that change happen within the bounds of a preexisting hierarchy will get you incremental movement. Understanding the social network within your organization gets you rapid and radical change."

Stephenson describes social networks as having the following human components:

- **Hubs** know the most people.
  They are among the most trusted go-to people in your organization

- **Gatekeepers** know the "right" people.
  They are human way stations. When information must funnel through one person on the way to another, you're looking at a gatekeeper. If this person likes you, he can be an invaluable broker. If not, you've got problems! Important: Hierarchies rely heavily upon this role, whereas Web-based networks and direct peer-to-peer collaboration often ignore this person. This paradox and tension are felt throughout many companies as they attempt to increase collaboration

- **Pulsetakers** know the most people who know the right people.
  (For example, "I've got a friend of a friend who says this is what's really happening.") Pulsetakers may have the least-direct social ties, but their observe-and-wait views affect the rate of change in many organizations

Stephenson uses NetForm's proprietary software to map the connections between these groups of people and to speed up the process. She says, "Extensive interviewing — enough to draw the right conclusions — is labor-intensive and expensive. We can now bypass that step by searching for patterns in the connections between people. It took 30 years of research to get to a 30-day solution, but we can now show a senior team a virtual X-ray of their firm in about a month." (This is the software that Steelcase licensed; see Chapter 4.)

The resulting visual looks like a spider web: hubs at the center of all activity, gatekeepers and pulsetakers farther away from the action. This graphic is likely to be different than your hierarchical org chart. For example, a senior vice president may be the gatekeeping head of a department, but when it comes to how things *really* get done, the social network map might show that someone three-deep in the organization is the actual go-to person.

Using the invisible workplace to improve business performance. Mapping your social network is a critical tool for Work 2.0 managers who need constant buy-in and commitment from employees. If you understand and work with the social structures within your company, you can speed up how you connect with people's hearts and minds.

For example, if your goal is rapid innovation and change — such as quickly implementing the next big initiative, or pulling new products through development phases in one-quarter the time — it is critical to identify the trusted go-to people in the social network. Engage them, transmit your knowledge and goals to them, and their influence on the network will spread the change for you.

Many senior execs shoot for this effect by broadcasting everything to everybody — in hopes of diminishing the impact of gatekeepers. By doing so, they will get messages deep into the social network. But constant broadcasting also violates a tenet of the new work contract: My Work My Way. Those go-to people in your network want more customized information. Everybody else wants less noise.

If you restructure your company or merge with another firm, social mapping can be supercritical. Says Stephenson, "We recently assisted a large multinational firm during a merger. The senior team informed us whom they were thinking of letting go, whom they were going to outsource, and whom they were going to retain. Upon analysis of their social networks, I came to the conclusion that some of their decisions were headed in the wrong direction. For example, they were keeping one manager but outsourcing his entire network when the true value he had to the organization was tied up in the network that he had built.

"So I said, 'Either don't outsource his network or don't keep him.' Because his value-add wasn't what he could do alone, it was his network," Stephenson concludes.

This is where the connection between the new work contract and understanding social networks becomes most clear. Right now, most companies create strategies and structures, and then plug people into slots to complete the top-down design. But if productivity truly is personal, if employees want you to waste less of their time, and if they want you to create My-Way tools, your plans and budgets must be based upon the invisible power within your social networks. You will have to make informed decisions about outsourcing, whom to keep, whom to promote, what to build, and so on — based on social bonds, not just corporate mandate.

This is reinforced by Mr. Attention, Tom Davenport. In a recent research paper for Accenture's Institute for Strategic Change, he wrote: "Treating all knowledge workers the same creates major barrier[s] to improving effectiveness....The first step to leveraging their performance is understanding [their] differences."[5]

The choice is yours. For now, don't get hung up on social network jargon (hubs, gatekeepers, pulsetakers). And please, don't jump right into tactics. (Do we have to use software? Must we hire outsiders — can we do this ourselves? How much is this gonna cost?)

Let's be brutally blunt about the choice you face. The real issue here has nothing to do with tactics, budgets, or learning about social due diligence. What it comes down to is power and the illusion of control. It's scary for many leaders to confirm that power in the organization lies somewhere besides a designated slot on an org chart. Lots of leaders would rather not know.

Natural human reaction! And a competitive liability.

Lack of due diligence on social networks clogs your ability to go faster and improve performance. How and why people connect with each other has far greater impact on how things really get done than your designs for who reports to whom. The social networks inside your company make *everything* work.

If you're serious about productivity and growth, get serious about creating peer-to-peer value. You can only do that if you choose to understand and track your invisible social workplace.

A Heads-Up

In the next chapter, we'll dig into extreme leadership: what makes a leader "extreme" and why that's important. As you explore that topic, think back to this chapter and the difference between a leader who would choose to pursue social due diligence and one who wouldn't. That difference defines extreme leadership.

It takes an extreme leader to have the courage to go after the business benefits in knowing where power in the organization really resides.

Biographical Factoid Quiz
Answers: a1, b1, c2, d2, e3, f3

P2P Survey to help you discover new ways to deliver value, page 110

Getting Started Tips, page 114

Discovering P2P Value: Who, What, Where, When, Why

Not surprisingly, when you respect life's assets (Rule 1: Embrace the Asset Revolution) and when you give people better control over their own destiny (Rule 2: Build My Work My Way), people tend to collaborate more!

The following questionnaire will help you discover opportunities for creating P2P value. It takes elements from the toolkits for Rules 1 and 2, and restructures them for P2P use.

Using this survey. Select a small (10 to 25 people) cross-functional sampling of employees. Ask them to complete these ten questions. Then, use the Leader's Guide below to analyze their responses. This survey doesn't cover all that is valued in P2P exchanges, but it's guaranteed to get you started.

P2P Survey

Each question asks for three responses. If you can easily list three different responses, please do so. But don't force it. It's OK to list only one or two responses. There are no "right" answers. Respond based on how you really get work done.

1. Competing on Clarity

Please list the three people who, most often, help you work smarter and faster.

a. _____

b. _____

c. _____

2. **Navigation**

   Whenever you feel lost, or you're searching for new information, which three resources (people or tools) provide the least frustration and the fastest answers?

   a. _____

   b. _____

   c. _____

3. **Fulfillment of Basics, and Speed**

   To get your work done, you need the right information, in the right way, in the right amount. Which three resources (people or tools) get it to you the fastest?

   a. _____

   b. _____

   c. _____

4. **Usability**

   Which tools, training, or corporate-supplied information (no people this time) are the easiest for you to use?

   a. _____

   b. _____

   c. _____

5. **Time**

   Which three resources (people or tools) are most respectful of your time and attention — using them wisely and effectively?

   a. _____

   b. _____

   c. _____

6. Relevance

List the three people whom you go to most often whenever you need help figuring out how a project or change is relevant to you

a. _____

b. _____

c. _____

7. Next Steps

List the three people whom you go to most often whenever you need help figuring out specific next steps — what to do next on a project

a. _____

b. _____

c. _____

8. Success

List the three people whom you go to most often whenever you need help figuring out how your work will be evaluated, and what success looks like

a. _____

b. _____

c. _____

9. Tools and Support

List the three people whom you go to most often whenever you need help figuring out which tools or support* are available to help you get your work done

*(training, technology, information, funds, people, etc.)

a. _____

b. _____

c. _____

10. WIIFM (What's in it for me?)

List the three people whom you go to most often whenever you need help figuring out what's in it for you if you take on a new project or change

a. _____

b. _____

c. _____

P2P Survey: Leader's Guide

Questions 1 – 5 focus on overall organizational effectiveness and ways to innovate faster. If your employees' answers closely match what you intended in your plans (they go to the intranet when they're *supposed* to, they go to their manager when they're *supposed* to, etc.), your plans are closely aligned with how peers really want to collaborate. If, however, their answers are different from what you had expected, *you have to change your approach,* not the other way around. The power of peer-to-peer connections will always trump corporate plans and logic.

Questions 6 – 10 focus on day-to-day implementation issues. Again, study the differences between employee answers and what you expected. In most companies, all the answers are *supposed* to be "my manager." The responses may differ — indicating those who create true value for your employees.

All Questions: Any people listed who are not "my manager" are social network hubs — they're the real go-to people in your organization. Look for multiple mentions of the same names. They create the most value for others.

DELIVERING PEER-TO-PEER VALUE

Getting Started Checklist

Do

Don't

---

1. Pay attention
If you are willing to let them, your employees will teach you what they need from you and what they find most valuable in peer-to-peer exchanges

Underestimate the power of the invisible workplace

---

2. Get more out by putting more in
Give people more real-time, exciting, useful, and addictive stuff to talk about, and they'll change how they collaborate

Confuse "empowering" employees to collaborate without you with the hard work it takes to create peer-to-peer value

---

3. Deal with the illusion of control
Mapping the invisible workplace may confirm that the org chart does not represent the real power in the organization

Bother if you're not serious

chapter 7

Rule 4.

Develop Extreme Leaders

> King Arthur: I am your king!
>
> Woman: Well, I didn't vote for you!
>
> Arthur: You don't vote for kings.
>
> Woman: Well, how'd you become king then?
>
> Arthur: The Lady of the Lake...held aloft Excalibur....
>
> Dennis: Listen, strange women lyin' in ponds distributin' swords
> is no basis for a system of government!
> Supreme executive power derives from a mandate from the masses,
> not from some farcical aquatic ceremony!
>
> **from the Ancient Archivists who say "Ni"**

The leaders of great workplaces accept accountability for life's precious assets

In the beginning, leaders prioritized, strategized, culturized, and energized people's hearts, minds, and hands. And it was good. The people rejoiced. Together with their leaders, they laughed, worked, and sweated.

Then one day, the people noticed that their leaders' fingernails no longer got dirty. They had forgotten what their work was like, and had removed themselves from the day-to-day challenges they faced. So the people stopped drinking the corporate Kool-aid, and started seeking extreme leaders. They wanted to follow a leader who truly understood what it takes to get everything done.

This is no fairy tale. It is real-world. And the message is critical to your ability to attract and retain more talented people who can get more done with fewer teammates.

The future of leadership is extreme accountability for life's precious assets. Part of the new deal is that your employees want greater returns on their assets — time, attention, ideas, knowledge, passion, energy, and social networks. (They learned this behavior — fighting for better ROIs — from you!)

What puts the "extreme" in extreme leadership is your willingness to be challenged on, and to address, work-level details. To partner with employees who have no fear about pushing upward. Who want you to understand risk-taking and work from a frontline perspective; who want better decisionmaking tools and more flexibility about how to achieve results. Who will not tolerate "loser managers," as IBM's Extreme Blue interns kindly labeled them. And that's just for starters!

Simply put, extreme leadership means accepting the terms of the new contract. It's a matter of acknowledging that the route to corporate success includes changing the path employees must take for personal success.

OBSERVATIONS FROM THE 2.0 CAFÉ

"I love what IBM is doing with Linux," said the email to Irving Wladawsky-Berger, IBM's reigning Linux guru and vice president of Technology and Strategy for their Server Group. The author, Robert Spanos, continued: "By the way, I've written a proposal to redo my high school infrastructure using Linux. Would you like to see it?" Spanos was 15 at the time.

The conversation that ensued between the two landed Spanos a spot on an Extreme Blue team, working side by side with MBAs and graduate-level technical students. (See Chapter 2 for more about the program.)

Jane Harper, head of Extreme Blue, mentions with a grin, "We had to wait until he was 16; then we could hire him." The paradox of working with an intensely brilliant temporary employee who is also a teenager amuses Harper. When CNN wanted Spanos to fly 3,000 miles to do an interview about Extreme Blue, his response was "Sounds great, Mrs. Harper. But I really have to ask my mom first."

Spanos's slightly older teammates were equally gracious, but were far tougher negotiators. These best-of-the-best students made it clear they were only interested in doing insanely great work, and that their tools and teammates also had to be best-of-the-best.

Harper reports, "One team of interns recently met with Bill Zeitler, the group executive for our division. The next day, Bill told me he had already exchanged three lengthy emails with them. They wanted to know about his career track at IBM, what the company could offer them after the internship program, and lots more. He was thrilled, by the way. He said their excitement was contagious.

"Now, this guy is one of the most senior execs in a $90 billion company with over 300,000 employees. These kids didn't care. They're gonna talk to anybody. Hierarchies don't matter to them. They have no problem letting us know that their input is extremely valuable on strategic issues. And they have no problem telling us what they think is right or wrong." Harper concludes, "We'd better get used to this."

Business Results and the Extreme Pressure to Perform

Even as the new contract emerges, many firms are dealing with crippling layoffs, hiring freezes, and tough times for job-seekers. Control of the process is certainly not in their hands. Heck, one car dealer in Nashville, Tennessee, is asking applicants to fork over $549 to cover interview and screening expenses. (Positioned as a "motivation and training session," the money spent is refunded if they are hired.)

Nobody's saying that fresh-faced kids know what seasoned managers know. Or that the new contract or dedicating yourself to extreme leadership puts employees, of any age, in charge.

Extreme leadership hands no one the keys to the kingdom. However, it is about deep listening, learning, and responding to the details that high performers push back at you.

Whether it's a 22-year-old who pushes for the latest in groupware technology, or a 52-year-old who sees gaping holes in your corporate strategy (even after the senior team comes down from Mount Olympus to promote it) you are hiring people who know as much as you do about knowledge work and decisionmaking, if not more. Your employees are under extreme pressure to perform, and many of them know what it's going to take to deliver the results you seek.

Good leaders focus on results. Extreme leaders put more of their political ass on the line for performance, because they are willing to have their views on what it takes to get work done questioned, challenged, and changed. They trust the bottom-up feedback they receive about performance-related issues.

The Ultimate Guiding Principle and the One Test

Even without worrying about this kind of feedback, your role has never been more demanding and complex. And it's only going to get tougher. The accelerated pace of change and the intensity of expected results will continue to force you to push authority and decisionmaking deeper into the organization.

How will you know if you are truly developing extreme leaders, or if you're just keeping pace with tumultuous change? Two ways to check...

- **Guiding Principle:**
  Extreme leaders constantly ask, "Am I doing enough to demonstrate that I respect and trust the people around me? Am I changing enough?"
  These questions cut to the heart of everything in this book. You must change fast enough so that the infrastructures you build, the hierarchies you establish, the tools you create — everything that employees use to get work done — demonstrate that you respect their time, attention, and energy. This is the first of five new accountabilities on the path to extreme leadership. (See sidebar on page 128.)

- **The Big Kahuna Test:**
  Extreme leaders constantly ask, "How far will we go to ensure that employees can control their own destiny?"
  The remaining accountabilities all relate to this question. It is one of those conundrums that can never be fully answered. There will always be trade-offs between cost and benefits to the company, as well as to the employee. But if you commit to extreme leadership, you are committing to forever wrestle with this question.

Here's an example of the Big Kahuna Test: RTEC, for
RealTime Enterprise Computing, is an up-and-coming new
technology. It links the information that exists within a company
with information generated by partners up and down the supply
chain. Financial, sales, marketing, HR, inventory — *all* —
information can be *compared in real time.*

Many firms will jump all over this technology because it
promises to completely eliminate lagtimes and blindspots in
their decisionmaking that would otherwise bite them in the
butt. (Think about Cisco in 2000. Despite having an extremely
sophisticated IT structure, they fell from their position as the
world's most valuable company partly because they didn't know
that tons of customer orders were canceled until it was too late.)

But will these same firms see the value in eliminating
blindspots and lagtimes for their *employees?* They don't like
being bit in the butt themselves, and want to control more of
their own destiny. How many leaders will commit to building
employee-centered versions of RTEC technology?

The choice isn't a matter of cost or technology. The raging
debate, and far more important discussion, is about how much
value you place on an employee's time, talent, and autonomy.
In many firms, an employee-centered RTEC system would
threaten the gatekeeping and enforcement role of mid-managers.
Employees would have access to realtime information from
across the company about changing schedules, priorities,
personnel — and possibly budgets — so that they could do
more to manage themselves.

Conundrums like this one define the territory of extreme
leadership. Assuming the technology proves itself, lots of senior
execs will sign up for RTEC. But only extreme leaders — who
are committed to meeting employees' workneeds as a way to
meet customer and marketplace needs — would sponsor an
employee-centered version.

As you can see, extreme leadership can create as many
challenges for you as solutions. So why go there?

Business performance, that's why. Implementation issues

always come down to two things: people needs and workneeds. Extreme leaders focus equally on both.

Extreme Trailblazers

The rest of this chapter offers the stories of Trilogy Software and the treasurer of Shell Chemicals, trailblazers in extreme leadership.

Trilogy Software is a privately held ebusiness provider for such firms as American Express, Hewlett-Packard, Lands' End, and Nokia. Founded in 1989 by CEO Joe Liemandt, the firm has seen the same tough times as all high-tech firms, recently laying off 340 people — one third of its staff. But, says Liemandt, "We're not scared of reinventing the company. There are a whole lot of skills we don't have, and we [will] bring in the people who have them."[1]

The Secret to Becoming an Extreme Leader

Extreme leaders seek two mentors. One half their age. One twice their age.

Seek out a 15-year-old, or 20- or 25-year-old. Not like GE did: having techno-geeks teach dinosaurs about the Web. That's bogus. Any young Turks worth their insights would slam an exec for such a narrow use of their talents. Instead, embrace what Oliver Wendell Holmes once said: "Pretty much all the honest truth-telling there is in the world is done by children." Throughout human history, youth (whether children or the next wave of new hires) have always spoken the truth to power. People with mortgages and 2.2 kids in college quickly forget how to do that.

At the same time, seek out someone who's 55, 65, or 85. Probe for wisdom, but sift carefully. As Matsuo Basho, the Japanese poet, once wrote, "Do not seek to follow in the footsteps of the men of old; seek what they sought."

Trilogy is developing extreme leaders in many ways. Most notably, its training function, Trilogy University, reinvented itself by pairing a potential client (Bristol-Myers) with its newest hires to prototype how Trilogy should tackle a new market. The client company and the new hires dealt with details most senior execs would have glossed over.

Extreme Times Call for Extreme Leadership

"Always work to replace yourself. Teach your leaders that their main priority is to energize and grow their team,"[2] says Joe Liemandt, head of Trilogy.

Nice sentiment. But this is a firm that just laid off a huge chunk of its talent. Is this just corporate PR? To find out, over a nine-month period I had multiple conversations with two of the people responsible for the nitty-gritty details behind Liemandt's vision. Jim Abolt is Trilogy's head of HR, and Allan Drummond runs the company's training unit, Trilogy University.

Abolt was brought in to Trilogy in 2000 to revamp whatever dot-com thinking remained in the organization. He's worked in a steel mill, a Frito-Lay plant, and, most recently, was vice president for leadership development at Bristol-Myers Squibb. Liemandt recruited him to direct the layoffs and bring discipline to Trilogy's leadership efforts. We first spoke shortly after his move to Trilogy.

The changing role of leaders. "One of the things I often hear is that, *everywhere,* it's just too hard to get things done. There's no question in my mind that if we help leaders see that there's an opportunity to create value by making things easier, they'll jump on it. Because really smart people like to create value. They hate getting hung up on things that don't add value.

"Employees in knowledge- and service-based companies do their work because they love it. Anything that gets in their way — whether it's lack of clarity, poor leadership direction, or cumbersome processes created by leaders who aren't focused on creating simple work environments — reduces the time they have to do what they love."

Those comments were made pre-layoffs and in the still-early days of a rocky economy. Does Abolt still feel this way? "Absolutely!" he says. "Now, more than ever, a leader's job is to ask, 'What do I do that creates useless noise or lack of clarity? What do I do that distracts people from customers? How could I do my job differently so that we can build a simpler workplace?' All leaders *must* focus on this!"

But paying attention to the workneeds of your troops — is that valid in a tough economy? Abolt's answer is as tough as a steel mill manager's. Immediately after the first round of layoffs, he announced to those remaining: "I can train a turkey to climb a tree. But I'd rather hire a squirrel." The best use of people's time includes knowing who is best suited to take the firm into the future, and who is not.

Smart extreme leaders only put more of their ass on the line for squirrels.

Getting extreme with customers. Allan Drummond was in the first Trilogy University (TU) class in 1995, and was then tapped to run it. His mission has always been to do more than just train and develop people. TU is the vehicle Trilogy uses to drive a cultlike connection to the company, and preach the spirit of innovation. Drummond and his team were so successful with this mission that TU was showcased in *Harvard Business Review* as the model of the future.

Then came an economic downturn. The kudos are still valid, but TU was quickly revamped to focus more on the customer. "We have a unique take on developing extreme leaders," says Drummond. "We were already too focused on our own culture, so we looked outside the company."

"We're inviting customers to teach us where and how our employees should spend their time and energy. All 50 people in each TU semester spend a quarter doing an on-spec project for a customer. It's a win-win all around. The customer gets our technical insights — cheaply! We build our relationship with them, and equally important we develop leaders who see deeper connections between marketplace needs and how we spend our employees' time and talent."

For the first project, Trilogy turned to one of Jim Abolt's ex-teammates. They asked Don Hayden, executive vice president of Strategy and eBusiness for Bristol-Myers, to share his toughest problem.

Hayden and his team presented Trilogy with a 30-year-old challenge that no one in the pharmaceutical industry has solved. In nonmedical terms, it's how to build richer, longer-lasting relationships, and thus revenues, with an installed base of customers (patients with chronic conditions, like high blood pressure or diabetes).

The challenge is that many people who really should keep taking certain drugs, don't — because human nature kicks in. Since their body doesn't provide immediate and visible feedback if they miss a dose or two, they figure they can stop taking medication altogether. Both medicine sales and patients' lives could be improved if Trilogy could help with patient compliance

Servant to the Details

Max DePree, former CEO of Herman Miller, wrote in *Leadership Is An Art*: "The first responsibility of a leader is to define reality. The last is to say thank you. In between, the leader is a servant." His views were greatly influenced by Robert Greenleaf, who, in 1970, developed the tenets of servant leadership.

Extreme leadership is nothing more than "in between, being a servant." With one important addition: The devil is in the details. Extreme leaders do the due diligence: They experience the systems, tools, and processes that employees are forced to use. They measure the effectiveness of work designs. They study and make use of the power in the invisible social workplace. And lots, lots more.

and persistence, and help patients see the effects of taking or not taking the medication.

So 50 TUers spent three months exploring the challenge from the patients', doctors', and client's perspective. By the end of their semester, they had prototyped an entire portfolio of possible solutions. Among them: completely overhauling Bristol-Myers's use of the Internet to focus on building relationships with patients; creating a wireless pill bottle cap that sends messages to a computer, helping both doc and patient track medication compliance; creating a computer-based avatar that uses realtime patient data to visualize the effects of taking/not taking one's meds; and more.

Extreme lessons learned. "The Bristol-Myers team loved what they got," says Drummond. "It opened technological avenues and opportunities they had never considered, as well as opening new opportunities for us to work with them. The experience also suggested a whole new way to look at the details of work. Instead of using spreadsheet analyses of resources, hours, and plans to make decisions, these new leaders lived and debated each choice. Then they got direct feedback from customers about the choices they made.

"We have overall goals of 100 percent customer success and 50 percent earnings growth. Everyone at Trilogy understands intellectually what that means. But it takes a lot for really talented, sometimes independent people — like we have here — to work out what to do to achieve those goals.

"Now," concludes Drummond, "we're getting much more customer focused, *and* we're working on the new contract." Joe Liemandt and his senior team are learning lessons from TUers about personal productivity and how to organize work — like the link between personal learning and development and new business development, the power of including the workforce in resource allocations discussions, the natural alignment that occurs when people get closer to the customer, and much more.

Knowing the value of extreme conversation. When the topic turns to communication, Jim Abolt is amazed at the difference between Trilogy and his past employers. "My God, I can't believe how much information these guys share." Trilogy lives another basic tenet of extreme leadership: Avoid no dialogue and fear no questions from the bottom up.

If you are like most leaders, extreme conversation will fall outside your comfort zone. You're used to dictating the terms, timing, and scope of key conversations. Under the new contract, that's going to happen less and less.

Imagine a really tough meeting with the top people on Wall Street. Think about how they would dig into your spending of shareholder assets, and how you would get dinged if you came ill prepared for such questions. You just visualized the kind of conversation that Work 2.0 employees expect. They are just as passionate about their investments in you, and will probe just as deeply.

Trilogy understands and embraces these conversations. "As part of our intranet," Allan Drummond reports, "we run a site called Leadership.com,[3] which provides leaders with productivity tools, like an organizational dashboard — discussion forums, streaming media, survey tools, and training modules. The open-forum conversations have generated both healthy controversy and improved focus among our employees. People feel incredibly free to ask whatever questions they have of our senior team, and they expect well-reasoned responses. Joe [Liemandt] and Jim [Abolt] have made it very clear that maintaining the dialogue on this site is part of every leader's responsibility."

Here's an example of a particularly tough conversation. "We recently started thinking about a new compensation plan, one that would change the mix of many people's pay," says Drummond. "For us, having the comp team go off and plan everything in isolation was never an option. Our employees would have told us, 'Hey, this is our company. Let's do this in the open!' So Joe and our director of compensation went

onto Leadership.com and answered questions like:
- 'Explain the incongruity between this plan and our retention efforts.'
- 'How much will the proposed plan cost or save the company?'
- 'How can you justify this when...'

"People wanted not only to understand the plan, but also to have a say in how it was designed. So Joe posted informal surveys asking for employee input. For example: 'Do you prefer a cash-rich or equity-rich plan?' The results of those mini-surveys became the guiding principles for the new plan.

"What makes us different from most other companies," says Drummond, "is that Corporate Affairs never scripted a

Developing Extreme Leaders

Everything you already know about leadership is still valid. Great leaders excite and inspire us, shaping our view of the future. They seek out, nurture, and keep great people. They set clear goals, communicate effectively, are self-aware, empower those around them, and focus on results. The path to extreme leadership includes **five additional accountabilities.**

Extreme leaders...

1. **Confront the extreme question, often.** Companies that develop extreme leaders debate and wrestle with this question at least quarterly: "Are we changing enough to demonstrate that we respect and trust the people around us?" Everything that employees use to get work done must ooze your respect for their time, attention, and energy. Making sure people feel appreciated and telling them that their work is important will always be part of your job. But now, respect is a whole lot bigger than that.

sanitized Q&A." The dialogue happened without filters, allowing managers and employees to break through hierarchies and attack the issues that mattered most to employees. Leadership.com even allows anonymous posting, a critical part of achieving Liemandt's goal of "feeling the pulse of the company."

With Leadership.com, Trilogy management moved discussions out of closed offices and into the open, where sensitive issues could be addressed and misunderstandings could be corrected. For example, some employees misunderstood the nuances of the new compensation plan. The open dialogue meant that their peers corrected them (and let them know they "weren't paying attention") rather than that animosity being

---

2. **Attend Extreme Leadership University.** The old model: GE's Jack Welch in the pit at Crotonville, going toe-to-toe with promising executives. The new model: Extreme University puts customers and frontline employees in the pit along with executives, pushing those execs into new demonstrations of respect. Whether it's electronically, as exemplified by Trilogy's Leadership.com, or in face-to-face exchanges, extreme leaders put themselves in situations where their views on what it takes to get work done will be questioned, challenged, and changed.

---

3. **Get their fingernails dirty, regularly.** Years ago, I learned an invaluable lesson from Pepsi. To be sure I understood frontline challenges, they wouldn't let me start a consulting gig until I spent a day delivering soda to grocery stores. I recently applied this lesson with the CFO of a globally known retailer. He spent a day as a cashier. He was shocked by what it took to make money in his stores. Extreme leaders are never shocked. They regularly participate in the business of getting things done and experience the company's systems, tools, and processes for themselves.

---

directed toward the senior team.

All of the dialogue on Leadership.com is just as boundaryless. Joe Liemandt has made it clear that Trilogy hires adults, and adults should be able to openly share confidential information and engage in healthy — sometimes tough — debate. Even a violation of trust did not squash this cultural norm. Thus, when an ex-employee anonymously posted confidential financial, sales, and customer information (some taken from Leadership.com) on an external message board, Trilogy didn't just shut down their site. The company took immediate legal action to have the information removed from the message board and to identify the individual, but they did not back away from their guiding principles.

---

4. **Seek extreme assignments.** Current career paths for up-and-coming executives include international assignments and responsibilities in different functions or business units. Extreme leaders are groomed by doing additional stints as the Fool (speaking the truth to power), as the New Quant Person (focused on work-design data), as the New People Person (developing user-centered tools and processes), and more.

---

5. **Redefine the exit rules.** Great leaders have clearly defined parameters for abandoning a strategy. They know when it's time to sell business units and when to lay off people. But extreme leaders get closer to the work. They pay more attention to details that high performers push back at them. Like when training and development are not keeping up, when the infrastructure can't handle the load, when resources are stretched too thin, and more.

Work 1.0 leaders were wimps if they considered these factors. Better to use brute force, and keep pushing until missed financial results said it was time to admit failure. Work 2.0 extreme leaders will be smarter. They'll know more about when failure is really occurring — long before the financials show it.

The rewards of passing extreme tests. Extreme leadership will push you out of your comfort zones. With tough dialogue. Learning from customers and new employees about how to spend your working capital. Making sure the people you count on for results know that you also care about what drives their time, talent, and energy. These are a few of the tests you'll face.

The rewards, however, can be equally extreme. The ability to get more from fewer people has never been more critical in a leader. As this book went to press, the economy was teetering on the edge of recession. Now consumer and market confidence are depending on you to do more than just push to meet targets. Any leader can slash headcounts, control costs, and drive for better business results. Only extreme leaders can do that *and* increase employee commitment.

"When events become too complex and move too rapidly, human beings become demonstrably less able to cope," said U.S. Federal Reserve Chairman Alan Greenspan during the 1998 financial crisis. "The failure to comprehend external events almost invariably induces disengagement, whether it be fear of entering a dark room or of market volatility."[4]

Consumers, investors, and your employees need you to break down more of the barriers that get in the way of getting stuff done. That includes your preconceived notions about what causes disengagement and complexity for workers.

Number Crunchers Can Be Extreme Too

Extreme leadership needn't involve outrageously innovative programs and organization-wide efforts. It can be just one person asking him- or herself, "Am I changing enough to live my own values?"

In an unscientific poll, I asked a few dozen friends to name extreme leaders they knew. Tom Kunz, assistant treasurer at Shell Chemicals, nominated his boss, Karim Hajjar, treasurer and Deputy CFO: "What makes Karim an extreme leader is how he focuses on what we need to do our job, as well as our personal development. In my entire life, I have never seen this level of trust and openness in a workteam."

The two work several thousands of miles apart, separated by the Atlantic Ocean. I'll let a series of emails between the three of us tell Hajjar's story.

Tom Kunz nominates Hajjar: "I have never experienced this level of trust and openness with any other leader. Karim makes things happen, yet he is vulnerable, humble, and willing to learn. Here's what I've observed within the past few months:

- He has nearly tireless energy (sometimes too much).
- He models how to work hard and play hard. He sets boundaries around personal time and keeps them. (He sees his son only on the weekends and therefore almost never travels on those days.)
- He's unbelievably genuine — no false pretenses or hidden agendas — and works hard to resolve conflict. (More than once, he's called me after a video- or teleconference to make sure any conflict in my mind was resolved.)
- He asks numerous people to coach him, including those of us who work for him. He genuinely wants to be better.
- He finds negotiating to be fun and challenging, but never knowingly at the expense of another individual. He never accepts anything without pressing boundaries.
- He's a doer, reflecting an extreme leader's need to get his fingernails dirty. That way, he really understands the work it takes to get everything done."

Hajjar's response: "Tom, your comments are very kind. I wish I felt as accomplished as you give me credit for being. But your comments are not balanced enough. There are quite a few negatives to mention. Such as my tendency not to allow people enough time and space to form their views; my tendency to react too quickly without checking that I have all the relevant information; and my tendency to focus most on the people I enjoy spending time with. I need to do more to respect everyone

I work with. One other thing: Your kind nomination is a little embarrassing. While I am truly flattered, I am also nervous about appearing boastful."

Kunz: "Karim is right on all counts. But his imperfections are why I see him as an extreme leader. The key is that he knows the areas he needs to work on, doesn't hide them, and works on them with his team."

Kunz follow-up: "Here's another example. The following is [part of] an email that Karim sent to a couple of us after a tough but important meeting:

'I want to thank you for helping me on a very important journey about value in the last few days. There had been a gulf between us in the recent past. This was not so much that we disagreed, but that all of a sudden, we each interpreted changes differently, and came to different conclusions. I know you guys were frustrated and pissed off at the conclusions I had come to.

'I was frustrated too. Not by your positions, but by
- The prospect that I was disconnected and out of touch with your views
- The fear that I had lost "control" by enabling you to lead so much on your own
- The fear that I had for your credibility within the organization if I couldn't persuade you to be more objective

These conditions made me more "difficult" and "narrow." So I'm pleased that you challenged me and held your ground, no matter how busy and frustrated you were. I want to thank you for helping me a lot!'"

'Nuf Said

Not every extreme leader will have the chance to rebuild an infrastructure or completely change a company. But every one can ask him- or herself, "Are my actions keeping pace with all the change that's coming at others, including my team?" You'd be well on your way to extreme leadership if you asked questions like this one as often as Karim Hajjar does.

Postscript

I would never presume that this is anything but a mere business book, and I know that I cannot do justice here to the events of September 11, 2001. I'm writing these words only shortly thereafter, and it may be years before we fully grasp the breadth and depth of the new changes swirling around us.

Yet one aftereffect is already clear: Most everyone is experiencing a new kind of wrenching uncertainty. Never before has your leadership been so critical. Never before has changing how you lead been so urgent.

We have entered a new era of uncertainty. You can't make it go away with better planning, strategizing, or communicating. Being profitable isn't a strong enough guarantee anymore. Everybody knows that their boss is just as clueless as everyone else about how to address issues that reach far beyond your corporate control.

But what people *can* control is how they choose to spend their time, attention, and energy. If anything positive comes out of September 11, it will be your employees' thirst for extreme leadership. You will have to do more to earn their time, their trust, their energy. And you will do more to ensure they have more control over their own destiny.

Also as we went to press: U.S. Navy SEAL Lieutenant Commander Rob Newson, who coined the term "extreme leadership," said, "We are preparing to do our jobs."

section

3.

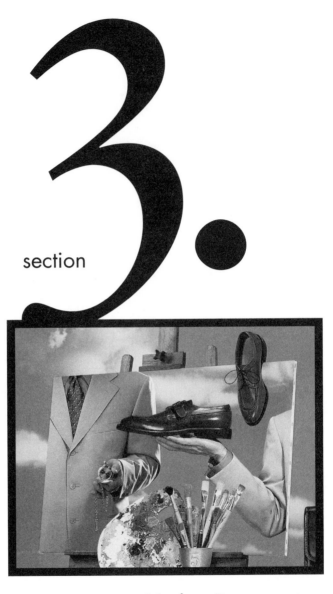

Under Construction

You have what you need

to get started.

These next chapters are seasoning
for the mix:
additional stories and signposts pointing us
in a new direction;
showing us the unfolding future.

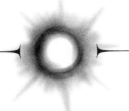

Surfer's Guide

The goal of this chapter is to add to the richness of the 2.0 experiences and voices you have already heard. During the research for this book, I met many people who had insights into the world of Work 2.0. Some have suffered setbacks; some are thriving. Sometimes they contradicted each other on where to focus, and other times they described tripping over solutions in the dark. Space does not permit me to relay all the stories I heard. What I can tell you is that the people who will move us into the new contract share a common view. They understand that in a Work 2.0 world, the basic concepts of value, community, and commitment take on new meaning.

Why My Work My Way will be embraced by every leader and why every leader must be extremely thoughtful about what happens next.

chapter 8

Short Takes

I am certainly not one of those who need to be prodded.
In fact, if anything, I am the prod.
Sir Winston Churchill

That so few now dare to be eccentric,
marks the chief danger of the time.
John Stuart Mill, *On Individuality*

A SAMPLING FROM THOSE WHO HAVE SEEN THE WORK AHEAD

Street Stories

Leila Sawyer, Extreme People Person
Supervisor, HMO Provider Services, Blue Cross

"*W orking in a beauty salon*
was my way of escape," says Leila Sawyer. "Ten years ago, I had just gotten out of an abusive marriage, and as I listened to other women talk about their pain, I found that I was not alone. While I did their nails, I just listened — because for five years I had no one listen to me.

"Most people just want you to listen, and not speak. So now, when employees talk to me, I listen. I am not too quick to jump in and give an answer because every conversation doesn't need a solution, just someone to listen."

When her own nail salon business faltered, she had no savings and no health insurance for her two kids. So she took a $6.50/hour job in a call center, and came to work in a business suit. "I believe a positive attitude about yourself is critical," she says. The first company she worked for recognized her abilities and threw more projects her way. But it wasn't glory work. One of those projects included working out of a closet, and redoing the company's paper-based filing system. "At first I cried in the bathroom lots of times, believing I was better than the jobs I was handed. But then I realized there was a bigger picture. I was learning how the company works."

Ever since, that has been her modus operandi: Learn how a company works by cleaning up their information systems. Use those experiences to move to something bigger.

Sawyer is now a mid-manager handling Blue Cross HMO customer calls, in an environment where you're evaluated by each call's "handle time" — how quickly you move on to the next problem. An environment where it's easy to get into a crank-it-out routine. Instead, she says, "I believe it's up to me to help each person grow every day they're here."

She loves being told she can't do things. "When I told management I was going to turn around the company's worst performers by spending more time with each one, they said, 'You won't have the time.' So I did it anyway." She turned the department around by giving individual coaching to each employee and by having all of them study tapes of their calls with customers. Within months, she astounded management when her group received a 99.5 percent Quality Assurance score. She had not only improved performance, her group had the highest morale in the place.

What makes Leila Sawyer an extreme leader goes beyond performance details. She understands the connections between the tasks people must perform and what will rock their soul. "Not everyone has the means to deal with everything thrown at them," she says, "but there's something inside every person here that's yearning to believe. I'm taking the whole group under my wing, not just one or two. They all deserve something to believe in. They all deserve more from me."

Shayne Lightner, Extreme Recruiter
Director, Executive Talent, idealab!

Before the tech wreck,

Shayne Lightner's bosses, idealab! cofounders Marcia Goodstein and Bill Gross, graced the covers of many business magazines. Idealab! was the model for how to run a business incubator. Times have changed: On paper, Gross lost gazillions of dollars. Like most tech-related firms, idealab! is struggling, but it still nurtures a network of about 40 companies. Lightner's job is to recruit the top talent for those firms.

"What I can speak to best," he says, "is what it takes to attract top-quality people. As an incubator, our business model is to lure people by offering them equity and a chance to run their own business. Even after the economy changed, we're still able to find those kinds of people. For some companies, stock options have become less of a driver. But the interest in some form of equity is here to stay. There's no way to erase the trends of the past few years. Employees want more of a say in how their businesses are run. So even if you don't see ownership in stock, you will continue to see the desire for ownership in how people want to participate in decisions that affect them.

"One of the biggest factors, that will never change, is that great people attract great people. Bill and Marcia continue to attract exciting people, nice and fun people, people who you just want to have a conversation with. For us, that's probably 60 percent of the recruitment game."

Is My Work My Way affecting his recruiting efforts? "Not so much at the senior levels in how it relates to productivity. But I *am* seeing how it relates to pay packages and equity. We're customizing everything to each individual.

"Probably the greatest indication I'm seeing of the new contract," he says, "is in the area of creating communities. The Internet definitely has changed how people connect with each other. I know we're able to retain our technology stars because of the efforts we put into building a community — within each company and among all the firms in our network. They come here for the community they couldn't build themselves."

Prior to joining idealab!, Lightner was a partner and managing director at Korn/Ferry International, one of the world's leading executive recruitment firms. So it's not surprising that he concludes with, "The war for talent ultimately is about who's at the top. If the company is run by smart, well-rounded, dynamic people, that's the kind of people they'll attract."

Sergey Brin, Extreme Googler
Cofounder, Google

*S*ergey Brin is the founder of one of the Internet's best-loved search engines. To stay light on his feet, his hobbies include the flying trapeze. In 2001, members of Women.com voted him runner-up for Internet Bachelor of the Year. He describes his biggest failure as trying to branch out too quickly and reach too wide as a young company. When asked how his mom would describe his Achilles heel: "She'd probably say I work too much."

Unlike Shayne Lightner, Brin de-emphasizes the role of his senior team and focuses mostly on the people who do the work. "We're just over 200 people now, so the accomplishments of this company are the accomplishments of each and every individual. I have had the greatest impact by hiring great people. The people who join Google have to work well with other people and be a pleasure to be around. And we've tried hard to hire a mix of people with diverse hobbies, interests, and skills. For example, one of our operations experts used to be a brain surgeon. Another used to work at JPL [NASA's Jet Propulsion Laboratory]. So I guess you could say that what we do here is rocket science and brain surgery."

When I asked Brin about leading according to the new contract, all his responses were akin to "Yeah, we do that," and then he immediately jumped back to talking about "great people." When pressed for details, he felt the best testimony to 2.0 work was an email sent to everyone in the company by Lucas Pereira, a recent new hire. The following are excerpts from that email.

"In honor of new Googlers everywhere, I thought I'd take a moment to write a beginner's guide to being a Googler. Alternatively titled, Why I'm Thankful to be a Googler.

- I have yet to meet a Googler I didn't like.
  If you need a hand, just ask. And you'll see how many helping hands are offered unconditionally

- I have yet to meet a Googler I didn't admire.
  Sit with somebody you don't know at lunch. Ask them what they've accomplished. You won't be disappointed

- Users email us every day, thanking us for our contributions. This really is a noble thing that we do — making information available to everyone, avoiding censorship, reducing clutter in their lives, and empowering them to feel good about the Net. In particular, read about the senior citizens who no longer feel intimidated

- Googlers are a brilliant, creative bunch, and tend to put some of their creativity on display. Check out Doug's headlines, Amit's clippings, Larry's scooter, Ed's toys, Ron's latte pictures, Heather's whiteboard, Schwim's penguin, the logging team's chainsaw, or the dozens of other funny things that fill the building

- Google got where it is today through the amazing efforts of everyone involved. From our founders to the people we hired last week, everybody has done their part. Don't take our success for granted; there is still a long road ahead

- Stop and smell the roses. Join the weekly hockey games. Where else can you shove your CEO into the bushes?

These are glorious times. Take a moment to remind yourself why we have so much to be thankful for.

Thank you all, Lucas"

Mike Wittenstein, P2P Innovator
IBM Innovation Accelerator

Wittenstein's insights are

representative of the sophistication about personal productivity, efficiency, and the performance of knowledge work that many of your employees will bring with them.

He attended high school and some college in Brazil, and finished his undergraduate degree in Russia. From there he did graduate work at Thunderbird School of International Management, launched a couple of software startups, and then landed at IBM a couple of years ago. He focuses on experience architecture: studying how all the parts of the company — brand, people, tasks, etc. — can be orchestrated to create positive experiences for customers and employees.

"It's amazing," he says, "what you see when you look at the experience through their eyes. With this new approach that focuses on people, we spot a lot of silliness and overmanaged activities. We can also create new roles and tools for employees to better serve customers, which, in turn, keeps the shareholders happy." From Wittenstein's perspective, the great news is that "the art and science of designing experiences are poised to explode! And there's lots of data embedded within those experiences that can help improve productivity and performance."

Each time we spoke, we were interrupted when UPS arrived to make a delivery: Wittenstein always has to have the latest gadget. As part of his job at IBM and for the pure joy of it, he's constantly trying out the newest technology and collaboration tools with an eye to making work easier for himself and colleagues.

He was one of the many people who toiled behind the scenes

to pull off IBM's 2001 WorldJam, a three-day online experience during which more than 52,000 IBMers brainstormed together. Some called the experience "the business world's online Woodstock." CEO Lou Gerstner likened WorldJam to Deep Blue, their chess-playing research computer, in its ability to help IBM develop mature product lines.

"There's so much to be learned from how people collaborate," says Wittenstein. He cites an example that reinforces the need to understand the invisible social network and the opportunity to benefit from mining the information that collaboration creates. "Just like detectives use phone logs to find out who tipped off whom, businesses (with the permission of their employees) can watch patterns emerge in peer-to-peer collaboration, then share them in realtime with others who face the same challenges. For example, if a customer problem always causes Joe to talk to Alicia, who talks with Marco, we can identify and nurture a best practice by what just went on. Solving that particular problem gets simpler."

He also sounds a cautionary note. "One of the keys to intense collaboration is user-centered design. This means major commitments from senior executives. For example, in WorldJam, lots of people had to be working hard behind the scenes so that 52,000 people didn't have to work hard to collaborate." Wittenstein reinforces that executives are going to have to put a lot more into collaboration in order to get more out of it. "It takes hard work to make things easy," he concluded.

John McCarter, P2P Curator
CEO, The Field Museum

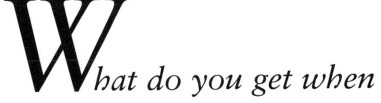

What do you get when
you combine an ex-president of a seed company, an ex-budget

director for the state of Illinois, an ex-White House Fellow, a trustee of the University of Chicago, a guy who likes talking about bugs, and a close friend of Sue, the largest known *Tyrannosaurus rex*? You get John McCarter. He heads the Field Museum in Chicago, a global research institution. The field part of their mission includes digs around the world and rain forest preservation programs.

We talked about the challenges of creating now, wow, and addictive learning experiences on a not-for-profit's budget. "A cornerstone of what we do," he says, "is the idea of multiple intelligences. From preschoolers to adults, everyone needs to be stimulated and learn on cognitive, emotional, and sensory levels. The challenge is how to create all of that on a large scale with limited funds. We have recently grown from 1.5 million visitors per year to 2.4 million visitors."

He can meet that challenge because everyone in the organization has a shared passion. "We've got about 630 people on staff. Every single one of them is a true believer. We are truly on a crusade to save the world, and everyone who comes in here has to buy into that. Once they believe, the hard work doesn't seem hard at all. The work itself becomes the reward for many of our staff members," he says.

"We use technology to connect people with the richness of our mission. Using satellite and Web technology, our folks in the field conduct continuous live demonstrations with school children. For example, during the fall, one of our archaeologists files a report every day from China. We call the program our Field Expedition Company. Last year, over 12 million kids participated. We also help teachers build lesson plans around the broadcasts and the databases we maintain."

Impressive numbers. But McCarter gets most passionate when talking about one teacher and one student. "A Teach for America team-teacher was struggling with one boy for several years. Even as a fourth-grader, he still wasn't engaged in learning. Then they came on a trip to see Sue, our T-Rex. After going through the museum, the teacher encountered her worst nightmare on a field trip — she couldn't find the boy. Racing through the museum, she found him with a group of kindergartners. 'This is Sue,' he was telling them. 'She's 45 feet long and 65 million years old.' He had become the expert, helping others. That's the magic for any teacher. And for all of us."

McCarter is describing the ultimate peer-to-peer value — where the learning and collaboration in an organization touches people in ways you never could have imagined. The future war for talent is in creating wow and addictive learning not unlike what McCarter and his team deliver to millions of people each year. No, you're not a museum. But your training and development modules are competing for the attention of people who have been to the Field Museum, or Disney World's Animal Kingdom, or any truly rich learning environment.

In a knowledge-based economy, you no longer just *manage* or *lead*. With every communication, with every transaction, with every structure you build, you are creating content that others will use to problem-solve. You need to create content and experiences that people want to share with others.

Signposts We've Seen

"Every day at 9 o'clock, we run a 21-minute meeting. It assigns accountabilities. It's educational. Mostly, it gets people what they need quickly — truly respecting their time."

David Tamburri, P2P Innovator
Screaming Media

"In a decade's time, teenagers will have their own built-in power to make governments and corporations listen to them."
Adrian Hon, P2P Revolutionary
Chairman of Youth Outreach, Mars Society

"As leaders, we need to be very conscious that we're here to serve the employees — making sure they can do what they need to do. I absolutely agree that My Work My Way is in our future. Complexity is growing more intense every day, and people will be extremely intolerant of sloppy leaders. They want work to be more customized so they can do their best. Also, I'm seeing employees pushing back on their leaders: 'Can we win?' They're asking, 'Why do I want to give up x-hours of my life for you? Are you worth it?'"
Janiece Webb, Extreme Leader
Senior VP, Personal Networks Group, Motorola

"If you don't respect people, nothing follows. If you do, everything follows. Respect includes everything in the work environment — removing the barriers that are in people's way. Respect also means including others in order to make executive-level decisions. I am constantly sharing my challenges with my scientists: 'OK, if this were your problem, how would you define it? How would you design the team, and what would success look like?' There are too many good brains out there for me not to take this approach."
Lina Echevarria, Extreme Leader
Director, Inorganic Technologies, Corning Sullivan Park Research

"Feedback is so critical. When it's not there, people's stress and discomfort go through the roof. When I focus on personal productivity, it's amazing how much ownership employees take!"
Craig Stevens, My-Way Advocate
Director of eCommerce and Operations, Hudson Bay Company

"Freedom. Balance. Control. These three things are the bedrock of what people are seeking. Regardless of what they do for a living, everyone I talk to is absolutely focused on these criteria."
Todd Lappin, P2P Activist, My-Way Advocate
Director, Community Interaction, Guru.com

"Being respectful of people's time is something that we live by here. No white noise. No fire drills just to make everything seem urgent. Our job as a senior team is to modulate the priorities. But to be candid with you, this is easier to write in a book than to do. This new contract is very hard work!"
Ron Bension, Extreme Leader
President/CEO, GameWorks

chapter 9

Work 2.1

Privacy Matters

[
I will not be pushed, filed, stamped, indexed, briefed, debriefed or numbered.

Number 6, *The Prisoner*
]

"*B*ob, could you come into

my office for a minute?" Bob didn't like the sound of that. Anytime the senior vice president wanted a closed-door chat, it meant something was up.

"There's no easy way to say this, Bob. I'm gonna to have to let you go."

Blindsided, Bob gasped for air at the same time he stammered, "Why?!? All of my performance reviews have been far better than anyone's!"

"Well, ever since we started tracking you online, I've noticed how many hours your manager has spent helping you solve problems."

"Huh?" was the best Bob could utter. He was clueless that this kind of measurement was going on, or that it mattered.

"Your coworkers, all of whom report to the same manager, use their online tools to do their problem-solving. Not you, Bob; you're needy! Last month, you used 12.79 hours of your manager's time. We also have a videotape of last Tuesday's team meeting where you asked a question that took 30 minutes to answer. Thirty minutes multiplied by the 17 people in the room....Do you realize how much that cost us?"

Bob started to object, but the SVP just kept going: "As far as the suite of tools we provided you — B-o-b! Tsk, tsk. Last

month you spent only 13.5 minutes on Tool A, 27 minutes
on Tool B, and only 2 hours on Tool C. Maria, on the other
hand, is exemplary. She's totally onboard and online with the
right tools, and only uses 1.4 hours of manager-time. So, it's
outplacement for you Bob, and a big raise for her! Don't let
the door hit you on the way out."

Sound far-fetched? Not at all. Granted, I exaggerated for effect.
But the underlying principles are very real. The baby steps
toward Bob's experience have already been taken.

Companies are watching the Internet sites that employees
visit and are tracking down I-hate-my-boss musings on outside
message boards. According to the American Management
Association, nearly 75 percent of U.S. firms keep tabs on their
employees by checking email, Internet, and phone logs, even by
videotaping them. That's twice as many companies as in 1997.

According to Management Recruiters International, 40
percent of the firms they surveyed used monitoring software.
Some use programs to watch keystrokes in real time. They
would know, for example, if an employee started to write
something nasty, damaging, or offensive, then changed his or
her mind, trashing it completely. To the employee, the words
never existed. To corporate thought police, someone just got
flagged as a potential troublemaker. Technology allows more
and more firms to push the boundaries of privacy and
employee/company rights.

But monitoring Bob's nasty thoughts or his use of
confidential information isn't the big story.

The real gold mine is in collecting data on him: using the
information he unknowingly provides about himself to manage
productivity and activities across the company. As you move
into My-Way customization and tailoring, you will be facing
some tough choices. You *must* exploit what you learn about
employees and their activities. It's the only way you'll be able
to stay competitive. However, you *must not* cross the line of
exploiting the trust employees place in you.

Weird scenes inside the gold mine. Here's how that conundrum will play out over the next few years:

- **Step 1:** Companies begin My-Way customization of information and programs for employees. They find it speeds up frontline decisionmaking
- **Step 2:** Customized tools and interactions provide more ways to manage employees than previously possible. Savvy senior execs see all the behind-the-scenes data that are being collected on employee activities, such as
    - What they use to make decisions
    - What filters they use to prioritize decisions
    - How they communicate priorities and action steps
    - How they delete email directives from executives without opening them, etc.

    More and more nuances of how people get work done will be exposed and become available for intense scrutiny. The brainstorming will begin: "Hey, you know what we could use this information for?"
- **Step 3:** After checking with Legal, the senior team discovers the law is on the company's side. Employees have no privacy rights or ability to control their own data when using corporate computers
- **Step 4:** Big Brother, here we come

Many leaders, on the basis of Step 3, believe that pushing the boundaries of what a company has the right to track is a nonissue. Most laws around the world do favor the corporation, not the individual. But privacy and control-over-data issues will whack you upside the head long before the law is changed.

You shouldn't look at these issues legally. Instead, ponder: Where do you draw the line for using information about employees in order to improve performance? Do not take this question lightly. Unless current corporate behaviors change and you take a new position on privacy, within the next five years you will experience a whole new bottom-up revolution. Employees will push back on how you use what you know about them.

A Short History of Corporate Behavior

"You already have zero privacy — get over it!" bellowed Scott McNealy a few years ago. With that quote, the CEO of Sun Microsystems became a poster boy for the idea that personal information isn't private anymore.

So far, most of the information that is being collected has to do with our lives as consumers. Abacus, a division of online ad agency DoubleClick, is one company among many that maintain databases on U.S. households. They track and sell information on what the people in those homes eat and drink, the cars they drive, the pets they own, the ages and number of their kids.

Selling your life's data is how Acxiom became a $1 billion company. This firm has spent 30 years compiling files on 90 percent of U.S. households. Years before you made any online purchases, you probably told them about yourself when you filled out a warranty card on a toaster or power drill. They use many such sources to create amazingly rich profiles. And, for a fee, they'll provide that information to help

Leaders: If Privacy Matters to You

Establish a policy. Clearly define the information you will monitor about employees, what you will and won't do with it, and what happens to it once an employee leaves the company

Communicate the policy. Broadly. Clearly. Often. Everywhere.

Give employees access to what you know. If you're watching their keystrokes, time, or activities, they have the right to see their own data

Monitor your own activities. As the potential for profits and cost-cutting increases, so does the potential for abuses and misuses. Your vigilance in policing this policy should be the same as protecting your brand. They are one in the same: symbols of who you are

private investigators to track down deadbeat dads, and Wal-Mart to stock its shelves, and Mercedes dealers to decide whether you are truly a potential customer.

Hertz and Acme Rent-a-Car provide a peek into the future of consumerism. They have already begun to monitor more of your actions, and penalize you for them. Let's say you are driving to a convention just outside San Francisco. As you pick up your rental car, you tell Hertz that you plan to stay in the bay area. Instead, you and your buddies blow off the business event and head for Yosemite National Park. Suddenly, a concerned voice comes over the speaker phone. "Are you OK? Are you lost?" The Hertz representative, monitoring the telematics system built into the car, noticed that you weren't where you said you'd be.

Hertz is currently using information you provide about yourself to perform real-time inventory checks, tracking

Workforce: If Privacy Matters to You

Hopefully, your leaders "get" it. Here's what to do in case they don't:

Use multiple email accounts. Conduct politically sensitive communication with teammates through personal addresses

Opt out. Study your company's privacy policy. If your gut tells you that control over your own information is not a win-win, trust your gut. Opt out.

Question, question, question. With every new technological advance, there are new opportunities for corporate misuses of your information. If they *can* monitor you, you *must* monitor them.

Even if your leaders do get it and care about your privacy, why should you still be concerned? Data spills! Eli Lilly recently exposed the identities of over 600 Prozac users. Imagine if an unintentional leak like that included your in-depth profile: your learning habits, strengths, weaknesses, foibles, and that nasty 1997 argument with the boss.

whether their cars have been stolen. Your privacy was weighed against what the rental firm had to gain by tracking you, and company needs won out.

Acme goes one step further by partnering with law enforcement agencies. James Turner, one of their customers, found this out the hard way. After renting from Acme, he returned his car and was handed $450 in speeding fines. While no trooper had stopped him, Acme's onboard system monitored Turner's driving habits and issued him real tickets. "They tracked me across seven states," he said. "My privacy was invaded."[1]

So far, few of us feel like Mr. Turner. We are not complaining about privacy issues in any significant way. Because, while we're inching closer toward troubling scenarios, so far the effects of losing control of one's own data haven't hurt too many of us.

This same lack of concern exists in the workplace because most people are not visiting porn sites or sending nasty emails. Most have little to fear from your corporate snooping — so far. Everything will change once you can see where the gold is. When you start using My-Way customized interactions to dig deep into what people do and how they do it, the good, the bad, and the ugly will come oozing out of your corporate culture.

This future is predictable. If there is any lesson we can apply to workplaces by studying corporate behaviors toward consumers, it is that you *will* use My-Way data to figure out how to boost profits and cut costs. It's a matter of *when*, not *if*.

The changes are also being accelerated by the events of September 2001. The population at large has shown a willingness to lose some privacy to ensure their safety. Having given up that freedom, you will face new, deeper scrutiny from the workforce. Safety and security are one thing. Further encroachments on privacy just so you can make an extra buck or two are something else altogether.

So you're facing a choice: Start now developing a strategy and policy toward the use of My-Way and other personal data — or play catch-up once your competitors beat you to it.

If you're serious about getting started, here are some guiding principles.

A New Era Emerges

"For you to be successful in this area, two things have to be true," says David Gilmour, founder and CEO of Tacit Knowledge Systems. "One: The infrastructure and the information it collects have to benefit the individual, not just the enterprise. Two: Employees have to believe and trust you when you promise number one."

Gilmour spends a lot of his time thinking about control of personal information. Tacit's software products extract tacit knowledge (get it?) out of day-to-day email conversations and online collaboration, making them explicit for all to share. Essentially: Snooping into employee exchanges for the good of all involved — helping everyone learn and collaborate faster. Current Tacit clients include Texaco and Hewlett-Packard.

Let's say one of your teams spends a lot of time on a specific customer problem, constantly emailing each other to figure it out. In other knowledge management systems, for the company to use what the team has learned, they would have to first document the problem, then list the actions they took, record the outcomes, and finally post them in the company's system. One of Tacit's products searches the team's emails for patterns — identifying both the people and information that were most critical to solving the customer's problem — and organizes the results for others to use.

Gilmour is passionate that culture comes before technology. "You might as well forget it," he says, "if you try to implement any technology like ours and haven't already earned the trust of your employees. The most fundamental guiding principle — and it's hard to come up with a close second — is that you have to design everything you do with the individual in mind. Everything revolves around how they perceive what you're trying to do, and how you'll demonstrate that you can be trusted. That's why the 'opt-in' aspect of our technology is so important.

"I've found that in most companies, it's not that managers aren't thinking about this. It's that they lose track of what it takes to create an environment in which individuals can do great things. They're beaten by other details around them that have nothing to do with technology."

What are those details? Gilmour brings us back to the invisible social workplace. "I believe that great companies always have two worlds within them: the engineered, designed processes that are formally established by the company, and the unstructured, improvised connections made by the workers. Anytime an employee uses a computer or electronic tool, he should first be able to accomplish a given task. But then he should be able to enrich his own profile of priorities and information, gaining new insights each and every day. These details — what companies can do to assist improvised connections, and how employees create new insights for themselves — need more attention."

Getting Started

If it helps to have a short checklist: First, make sure you have a privacy policy that defines exactly what the company will and won't do with information gained about employees, and what happens to that information when an employee leaves the company. Second, Make sure your employees have as much control over and as much to gain from information about themselves as you do.

But the real list of to-dos runs throughout this book. If you are going to mine data generated by employee conversations, collaboration, and activities — and still attract and retain people — you'll need to live the ideas in this book. Be an asset revolutionary. Build My-Way tools that benefit the individual. Create peer-to-peer value. Exhibit extreme leadership.

As David Gilmour says, "We need leaders who exhibit both vision and restraint. People's behaviors and expectations are that their knowledge, and information about their activities, are very personal. Any environment that respects these views is already most of the way there. Any efforts that appear to employees to be invasive or interfering will end up backfiring in a variety of ways."

Endnotes

For lots more resources, tools, and chatspaces dedicated to Work 2.0, please visit this book's e-companion: **www.work2.com**

Chapter 2

1. *Yahoo Internet Life*, August 2001, page 102

Chapter 3

1. *Fast Company*, January 2001, page 106

Chapter 6

1. Tom Davenport and John Beck, *The Attention Economy* (Harvard Business School Press, Boston, 2001), pages 3 and 8
2. Ibid, pages 110–111
3. From case study, "Dell Computer Corporation: A Zero-Time Organization," 1999, by Dr. Keri Pearlson and Dr. Raymond Yeh of the University of Texas at Austin
4. *Wall Street Journal*, September 20, 2001, page 1
5. "Art of Work," Accenture Consulting, August 28, 2001

Chapter 7

1. *Austin* (Texas) *American-Statesman*, June 10, 2001
2. *Fast Company*, March 2001, page 95
3. You can view the open-to-the-public version of Trilogy's site at www.leadership.com. All discussions mentioned in this chapter are from Trilogy's password-protected, proprietary version.
4. "Worldwide, Hope for Recovery Dims," *Business Week*, September 24, 2001, page 43

Chapter 9

1. "Big Brother Knows You're Speeding," *Wall Street Journal*, August 28, 2001, B1

History of Work

1. For much of this list: many thanks to Bernard Grun's *The Timetables of History*, Simon and Schuster, The New Third Revised Edition. Grun provided all accurate timeline facts. All distortions are mine. (Someone fed me the first entry in the timeline, now I can't find that email. Thanks anonymous!)
2. http://www.uriah.com/apple-qt/1984.html
3. Robert B. Reich, *The Future of Success* (Alfred A. Knopf, New York, 2001), pp 7, 9
4. Institute for the Future 2001 Ten Year Forecast, page x
5. Project Y Summit, March, 2001

Acknowledgments

Thanks!

Take your work seriously,

but never yourself.

Dame Margot Fonteyn

Anytime I took myself or my ideas too seriously, these people made sure I stayed true to you, the reader.

Family. Last Father's Day, my son, Ian, whittled a little boat for me, the *Simplicity*. And throughout the year, my wife, Louise, tolerated file boxes of research clippings stored all over our house. I guess they've grown accustomed to this passion of mine. Thank you Beez and Ian for your time and patience. Thanks for your laughter, support, love, and selflessness.

My mom passed away in 1994, and my dad in 2000. I continue to be grateful that I was raised to follow my passions, creativity, and values.

Work-in-Progress Readers. Somebody had to slap me around when I was the only one who thought my babblings were clear and coherent. These wonderful people provided that necessary service: Mary Ann and Eric Allison, Michael Ayers, Jim Botkin, Julian Chapman, Tony Cortese, Marilee Goldberg Adams, Ian Hendry, Ira Kasden, Joe Katzman, Mark Koskiniemi, Tom Kunz, George Lixfield, Chris Macrae, Chris O'Leary, Laura Podlesny-Bastida, Greg Pryor, Rick Ritacco, Jim Shanley, Tony Welsh, and Andrea Zintz. Thanks guys!

Book Teammates. No one could ask for a better editor than Nick Philipson! He provided an environment in which I could thrive. Lots of latitude, but never too much. Thank you so much, Nick! And I wish everyone who reads this book could meet all the wonderful people behind the scenes at Perseus. They make writing a book both rewarding and exciting. Elizabeth Carduff, Chris Coffin, David Goehring, and Lissa Warren: Thank you!

Before Nick saw them, every draft of every chapter would go to Lisa Adams, my agent. Each time, the draft would come back with 75 percent red "suggested changes." If anything in this book is compelling and clear, Lisa deserves the kudos. I was just along for the ride. Lisa, you're the best!

Design and Production. With the humor and patience of a saint, Aimee Leary at Final Art took my scribbles and turned them into wonderful page designs. Mark and Matt Versaggi worked tirelessly on the e-companion site, www.work2.com. Mark Kozlowski, an old best-buddy, created the terrific photos in this book. Alex Camlin supplied our great cover and Marco Pavia oversaw pre-press production and printing. Nancy Hall dotted every "i" in the copyediting process and Melissa Grella checked into all the permissions we needed. These are the talented people who turned my words into a product that could be enjoyed and used. I'm extremely grateful to each of you. Thanks!

Book Interviewees. Cartoonist Gary Larson once drew an image of a professor at a chalkboard filled with hundreds of scientific equations. At the very end of all this deep thinking, the professor wrote on the board, "And then a miracle happens." In the proposal stage, I must have seemed like that professor to Perseus. Hundreds of people filled in the blanks in my outline by generously answering my phone calls and emails, and letting me bug them in person. Thanks to each of you!

Inspiration. One of the endorsers of my previous book kindly referred to me as "the Studs Terkel of knowledge workers." If only that were true. Terkel is an awesome radio host, journalist, and chronicler of the lives of Jane and Joe Workforce. If you haven't read his *Working* or *Voices of Our Time*, do so immediately! Like Terkel, I am inspired by the amazing things that Jane and Joe do every day. Booksellers will file this book under categories like "management" and "leadership." That's unfortunate. Workers deserve their own category. The front lines are where the real business heroics and stories occur.

Subject Index

👉
People Index, page 174
👉
Organizations Index, page 175

A

Accomplishment
  human dimension, 1–2
Account Manager Learning
  Environment (AMLE),
  100–102
Accountability, 20–22
  extreme, 53
  extreme leadership,
  128–130
  leadership, 27
  new, 31, 56, 83, 88,
  89, 103
Alice in Wonderland, 60
Alignment, 74, 91, 126
Asset revolution, 31–36,
  53, 189
  discussing what matters in,
  74–76, 79
  embracing, 66–79, 194
  meaning of, 31
  measuring what matters in,
  71–74, 79
  observing what matters in,
  69–70, 79
  questioning with, 60
  SimplerWork Index for,
  73–74, 77–78
  workplace respect as,
  67–69, 76

B

Baby boomers, 189–190
Behavioral change, 93
Beliefs
  importance of, 142
  ripping up, 26
Boot Camp, 86

C

Cafeteria-based compensation
  plans, 39
Capital, 34
Career management
  diversifying of experience
  and, 32
CEO Summit, 26
Challenges, 4
Change
  keeping up with rate of,
  29–30
Clarity, competing on, 20,
  77–78, 110
Coaching, 86, 142
Collaboration, 44, 70,
  95–98, 102, 147, 149
Communication, 91, 143, 154
  globalization, teaming
  skills and, 187–188
Community-based planning,
  72

Assets. *See also* Working
  Capital
  length of investment of, 57
  management's use of, 15
  people, 8, 14–15, 25
Assignments, extreme, 130

Companies
  customer information
  tracked by, 156–158
  employee communication
  tracked, 154
  homework on, 61
  simpler, 59, 92
  use of, 16
  workplace, my work my
  way for, 82
Compensation, 86, 127–128
Competing on clarity, 20,
  77–78, 110
Competitors, 19
Compliance, 89
Consolidation, 43
Contract, new
  accepting terms of, 118
  circulation of, 61
  evaluation of work in,
  18–19
  humor in, 19
  individual, value and, 17
  learning and, 18
  making of, 27–29
  meritocracy with, 55
  passion in results in, 16
  peer-to-peer connections in,
  17
  people's assets in, 14–15
  practical tools, 17
  simplicity/common sense
  in, 19
  starting with individual, 20
  three-way winning in, 16
  timebandits ignored in, 19
  trust, clarity, conversation
  in, 19

Subject Index

Subject Index

People Index

Organizations Index

Organizations Index

The History of Work

55 disruptive moments

pushing us into the new contract

[
The dogmas of the quiet past are inadequate
to the stomy present.
The occasion is piled high with difficulty,
and we must rise with the occasion.
As our case is new, so we must think anew and act anew.
We must disentrhrall ourselves.

Abraham Lincoln
]

65 million years ago

1. Dinosaurs become extinct: insufficient collaboration, knowledge sharing

100,000 years ago

2. Homo sapien Gork discovers fire: Hierarchies and power struggles begin

30,000 years ago

3. Cave paintings: Creativity meets capitalism (admission: two shells)

999–500 B.C.

4. First executive suite: Tower of Babel

5. Human wisdom reaches a zenith: Confucius, Buddha, Zoroaster, Lao-tse, Jewish prophets, Greek poets, artists, philosophers, scientists

6. Babylon launches first banks to capitalize on all the innovation

499–0 B.C.

7. Julian calendar of 365.25 days adopted, workweek finalized: 24/7/52.18

A.D. 0–500

8. Bound books replace scrolls: Librarians resist. Change management consultants brought in

501–1000

9. Chinese invent paper. Longest-kept competitive secret; Europe remains in the dark for about a millennium. **10.** Also invent book printing: Lawyers eventually sue some guy in Germany

11. Workday speed is reengineered: Horse-changing posts established for French royal messengers

12. Castles become first corporate campuses

1001–1500

13. First mechanical (water-powered) clock appears in Peking

14. Global brand management begins: Denmark adopts first national flag

15. Performance management begins: Inquisition uses tools of torture

16. Robin Hood begins first workplace benefits program, instant hit with rank and file

17. First pure-play dot-commers, called Alchemists
18. Gutenberg heard to exclaim, "This will be the biggest thing since the Internet"
19. Leonardo da Vinci invents parachute, instant hit with senior execs
20. The symbols + (plus) and − (minus) first come into use
21. First infotech standards war: Book publishing splits into separate industries — foundry, printing, and bookselling

1501–1983

22. Niccolo Machiavelli, world's first HR director
23. Shakespeare launches leadership development series: Henry's, Richard's, Titus, John, Julius, Macbeth, Hamlet
24. First water closets appear
25. Galileo Galilei faces Inquisition for heresy: Business success revolves around employees, employees revolve around top-notch leaders
26. Peter Minuit buys Wall Street and Times Square for $24, eventual home of global trading (colonials' use of Spanish pieces of eight are why stock quotes are in eighths, not tenths)
27. Business drug-of-choice on streets: first coffee house opens in Oxford
28. Joseph Guillotin invents better way to cut under-performing employees
29. James Watt perfects steam engine, which eventually leads to entire Industrial Revolution
30. Samuel Morse **31.** Thomas Edison **32.** Alexander Graham Bell have pet projects
33. 10-hour workday established in France (What happened to that?)
34. Night-shift work for women banned internationally (Ditto?)
35. Idea of a "week-end" first takes hold in America
36. Execs hire Frederick Taylor to get things back on track
37. The first "war to end all wars," like the next one **38,** radically alters production methods, standards for innovation and efficiency
39. Wall Street spinmiesters call October 29 a "correction"
40. ENIAC (Electronic Numerical Integrator and Computer) computes WWII firing and bombing ranges: Info Age is born at University of Pennsylvania
41. Same year we read Jack Kerouac's *On the Road*, the U.S. forms ARPA (Advanced Research Projects Agency), which begets ARPANET, which begets the Internet

42. One year before Woodstock music fest: Office of Charles and Ray Eames shatters the myth that, boo hoo, it's too hard to connect the individual to a complicated business landscape. Their mind-blowing film about the universe, *The Power of Ten*, creates the model for making the connection — frame of reference must always begin with the individual

43. Alvin Toffler's *Future Shock* foretells the dark side of knowledge work. Predictions of information and choice overload eventually come true, causing far more root-cause problems than execs care to admit

44. *All in the Family* does more than change TV. It forces deep social issues out of buses, farms, and lunch counters, into the workplace; Archie's chair is modern-day birthplace of diversity effort

45. MTV does more than plant its flag on the moon. It exemplifies the best and worst of how people and ideas come together during the next two decades. At the same time it emphasizes packaging over substance, eye candy over true illumination, and adds to society's attention deficit problem; it also grabs our human soul by exciting, entertaining, and shocking us. Managing the tension between those extremes will be a constant challenge in Work 2.0 workplaces

46. A meter is officially defined as the distance light travels in 1/299,792,458 of a second. Senior execs wowed. Take corporate speed and measurement systems to anal-compulsive levels[1]

1984–PRESENT

47. **Super Bowl Message Signals the Beginning of the End**

"Today, we celebrate the first glorious anniversary of the Information Purification Directives. We have created, for the first time in all history, a garden of pure ideology. Where each worker may bloom, secure from the pests of any contradictory and confusing truths. Our Unification of Thought is more powerful a weapon than any fleet or army on earth. We are one people. With one will. One resolve. One cause. Our enemies shall talk themselves to death. And we will bury them with their own confusion. We shall prevail!"[2]

While it may sound familiar, this quote did not come from your last quarterly meeting. This 1984 Apple commercial (with homage to George Orwell) foretold of the coming power of the individual. Outrunning storm troopers, past mindless masses, the heroine sent her message by hurling a sledgehammer at Big Brother.

When that commercial first aired, e-power among the masses was limited to little more than producing reports, spreadsheets, and kludgy artwork. Senior execs still had all the real tools. No need to share power or control.

Since then, the Internet and all its killer apps — like email and the still-evolving forces of mobile, wireless, and wearable worktools — have transformed how many people can empower themselves. Today, this includes most every knowledge and service worker.

According to a recent study by McKinsey, freedom and autonomy ranked equal to, or higher than, compensation in job-interview questions. McKinsey also found that in order to attract and retain the key talent in highest demand, companies will need to create more opportunities to affect company decisions, build businesses, and share in wealth creation.

It may have taken two decades to warrant attention, but the end of Work 1.0 began one Sunday in 1984. Now, the people with the sledgehammers have reached critical mass.

48. **Success Gets Complicated and Confusing, Forcing New Choices**

Both employees and employers are now wrestling with mind-boggling change, daunting and confusing decisions, in less time, with fewer and fewer how-to's. All of this makes it really hard to keep a consistent view of success for more than a nanosecond.

"There's no diabolic plot here," said Robert Reich in *The*

Future of Success. All the confusion and change are generated by what we want as consumers. "The easier it is for us as buyers to switch to something better, the harder we as sellers have to scramble in order to keep every customer, hold every client, seize every opportunity, get every contract. As a result, our lives are more and more frenzied," he stated.

"We can, if we wish," Reich continued, "reassess our standard measure of success. We can affirm that our life's worth isn't synonymous with our net worth....We can, if we want, choose fuller and more balanced lives, and we can create a more balanced society. The question is: Do we really want to?"[3]

The answer: Many high-performing people *are* choosing to reassess their measure of success. There's no diabolic plot here. It's just easier to focus on one's personal success — however it is defined — than to keep up with the fluctuating versions promoted by your company. Reich put it this way: "As our earnings become less predictable, we leap at every change to make hay while the sun shines."

This plays out in multiple, complicated, conflicting ways. Even though a rocky economy is keeping people from job-hopping, they're not getting greater rewards, recognition, or personal growth for sticking by you — just more work with fewer teammates. You may be cutting costs, but they see My-Way tools and other portions of the new contract as the only way they can deliver the returns you seek *and* take greater control over their own destiny.

49. **Let's Face It: Nobody's Investing Enough in Mid-Managers**

First, Break All the Rules was based on a Gallup study that established that a person's immediate boss has a bigger impact on employee satisfaction and retention than pay or benefits. According to a Spherion/Lou Harris Associates study, people who are unhappy with their immediate manager are four times more likely to leave than those who are satisfied with their bosses.

Now, how good are most companies at acting on those findings? A recent Linkage survey discovered that when HR execs were asked about the effectiveness of their leader and manager development efforts, 72 percent ranked their companies from "fair" to "needing significant improvement."

Today's mid-managers (the ones who are left) have the most complex role in your organization. Few companies are doing enough to help them develop all the skills necessary to deliver on business targets *and* keep customers happy *and* retain your key talent. Since fewer managers are around with the skills and tools that are needed, My Work My Way and the creation of peer-to-peer value become even more important.

50. **Customer Satisfaction Tanks, Teaches Talent Valuable Lessons**

You feel it when you're the customer. We all feel it. Sure, there probably have been a few moments when you've been truly delighted. But mostly, unless you're paying for high-end service or you shop in a really small town, customer service continues to deteriorate. With no end in sight. The economics of the times are forcing most companies to automate, offload service onto the customers themselves, or have them pay for it à la carte.

Surprise! There is a direct connection between the decline in service and the new attitudes you see in the war for talent.

One hundred percent of the people you most want to work for you also buy things. A couple decades of decreasing service paired with increasing competition for their ears, eyes, brains, hearts, and money have taught them they get more if they push back.

In its 2001 ten-year forecast, *New Consumers Creating a New Marketplace,* the Institute for the Future says: "The key insight we have gained...is that [more discerning, sophisticated or affluent] consumers use information differently. They search...in more channels, they prefer information [that enables them] to initiate contact, they use information to experiment more often...they are learning the value of their own personal information."[4]

The very things you love about the people you most want to hire — self-directed, driven, able to think on their feet, etc. — make them tough consumers. When they buy stuff, they are more demanding, know what they want, and will walk away faster than others when they don't get it.

These same people *do not* turn off these attitudes and needs when they come to work. If you think that's unfair — that, as employees, they should be more understanding and patient — you just don't get it. You are leadership roadkill. (Workforce to roadkill: "If you'd like a refund on this book, please call our customer service center. Your call is important to us. Please hold. All of our operators are busy.")

51. **Globalization: It's Really About Communication and Teaming Skills**

There are gazillions of global issues that affect how far and wide you will have to reach in order to compete effectively. A small sampling:

- According to the Hudson Institute, in 2000, the U.S. ranked 14th in terms of 24-year-olds with tech degrees. Russia, Finland, the UK, Singapore, and South Korea have the most
- According to Standard and Poors DRI/*Business Week,* at the current rates of change, China's output per person will surpass that of the U.S. in 2078

But these issues, and almost all that cite global statistics, are from the marketplace's perspective. Let's take it closer to the individual.

In order to ensure speed, efficiency, and productivity, it is becoming commonplace (for your competitor, if not you) for a worker in Zurich to hand off information and projects to a teammate in Los Angeles, who hands them off to someone in Singapore. All to ensure 24 hours of worktime within a 24-hour day.

If you are not intensely focused on how you add value to peer-to-peer connections, how will these knowledge workers master those handoffs? The get-your-fingernails-dirty view of globalization must focus on how you build new skills and create new levels of communication, conversation, and connections.

21-year-old Jennifer Corriero has built a global organization on this premise (see Chapter 2). She connects and mentors people in over 70 countries. When speaking to audiences she asks a powerful question: "If you were given all the resources you needed to do whatever you wanted to do, what would you do and what would you need?"

Answer: Most people say they would still need to enhance how they connect and partner with others.

52. **Welcome to the 30/8.75 Society**

24/7? Fuhgedaboudit!

MTV Networks/Viacom recently completed a study of 4,000 24-hour time use diaries. Americans four years old and up were included. Once simultaneous activities — like sending an email and participating in a teleconference at the same time — are factored in, we've extended our week beyond 24/7 boundaries.

"We have figured out a way to lengthen our day by six hours," reports Betsy Frank, who's in charge of research and planning at MTVN. She describes this phenomenon as behavioral convergence.

Six more hours makes for 30-hour days, or 8.75 days compressed into a normal week. Welcome to the Asset Revolution! People know they're being pulled in too many directions, that their work suffers, and they're not paying enough attention to what really matters. So they only want to work in places that value their time and attention.

53. **Gen Y Kids Come of Age As Boomers Say Adios**

In the U.S. alone, every seven seconds another person turns 50. At the same time, the first wave of 80 million kids born between 1977 and 1997 are joining the workforce. This is creating a schism the likes of which you've never seen!

On one end of the taffy-pull are intense worklife issues like eldercare, college education fees, and major shifts in life needs. On the other end: For the first time ever, business is hiring a workforce who grew up on mass-market, user-centered experiences. This includes everything from games and entertainment to education and shopping. Unlike any generation before, they will not accept anything but user-centered worktools and information.

While most companies will have to cope with cross-generational pulls, Gen Y — also known as Net Geners — will exert out-of-proportion demands for My Work My Way and Peer-to-Peer Value. They will make up an out-of-proportion number of your dreamers, dissenters, rebels, and institutional anarchists — which is true of any new generation. But more than any others before them, the Net Generation will be filled with trainers, not just trainees. They bring with them far greater sophistication about the design of knowledge work, and more ways to bypass Big Brother decisionmaking than Gen X or Boomers.

Those who had less access to technology will still challenge the way you do things. I recently had the privilege of hosting a Gen Y panel discussion that included 16-year-old Joy Love Hester. She comes from inner-city Pittsburgh, where gang fights and 20 percent pregnancy rates are common among her classmates. She warned an audience of HR and line managers: "You are ignorant. Because you *ignore* all the ways you could help us, so we can eventually help you." She's right. Today's mostly-Boomer managers are so fixated on short-term results, we've ignored what's right around the corner.

David Bunnell, CEO of Upside Media and head of their Project Y Summit, notes: "The more I look at this...segment, the more I realize how all my preconceived notions are wrong. Young people have a lot deeper understanding and are a lot smarter and more discerning than I ever could have imagined. It's a real challenge to reach this group."[5]

Are you ready to change enough to reach, attract, and retain Gen Y?

54. **Rocky Economy Raises the Bar for Leaders**

New hires coming in with new ways to design knowledge work. Poor development of mid-managers. Employees being trained, as consumers, to expect customized, tailored interaction....And all the rest. These factors do not go away during a rocky economy. News of layoffs and cost-cutting does not change whether or not these forces exist. Just how they come together.

When you combine a tough economy with all the disruptive moments that are behind the new contract, the pressure whipsaws back at leaders. You need to figure out how to leverage these forces to produce enhanced productivity. Fast.

55. **September 11, 2001...**

FAQ

THE MOST FREQUENTLY ASKED 2.0 QUESTION

"I thought I was in charge again. Is this for real?"

Dear Loony Author:

Are you nuts? Have you read the papers? Employees are in no position to ask for anything but breadcrumbs. As far as I'm concerned, there's no way that My-Way is coming our way.

Sincerely,

Exec-in-Charge

Dear Keen-Eyed Exec:

Thank you for providing the missing piece of the puzzle! After all the research and interviews I did for this book, one pattern in responses had me stumped.

I heard the exact same quote from no less than 21* senior execs in successful companies: "Don't tell anybody, but I'm glad the economy slowed down. At least now I'm back in control."

I have to admit, Keen-Eye, I didn't appreciate how tough you had it before the economy tanked. It must have felt horrible losing more and more control to empowered employees. Good thing we're experiencing a correction, eh?

Now I get it. Thank you for teaching me that tough economic times are really about control, not profits. And that "employee" should never be paired with ideas like "investment," "assets," or "ROI."

Gratefully yours,

Loony Author

work 2.o

ONE-PAGE SUMMARY

Why You Need to Read this Book

Today's economic shock waves are hitting more than your sector and your business. The rules of work have also been rewritten. Wrenching uncertainty for your employees has not disguised the fact that you are using their time, attention, and energy as working capital to meet your short-term obligations. They know it. And your best talent is seeking more in return than just a job.

Work 2.0 lays out four beacons for 21st-century leaders. These rules are hardwired into the nature of knowledge work. The key premise is that the people you most want to keep care deeply about these rules. They are watching, but not waiting, to see what you will do.

1. Embrace the Asset Revolution

Employees are seeking daily/weekly/monthly returns on the assets they invest in your company — namely, their time, attention, ideas, passion, energy, and social networks. The new war for talent will be fought over who provides the best returns on these investments.

2. Build My Work My Way

Business must focus on personal, not just organizational, productivity. The future of work is customized, personalized, and tailored to each individual.

3. Deliver Peer-to-Peer Value

Your employees are setting new standards for collaboration without you. Leaders must do more than get out of the way of those exchanges; you must add increasingly greater value. That means bottom-up criteria will drive more and more of your collaboration budgets and strategies.

4. Develop Extreme Leaders

The future of leadership includes greater accountability for performance through greater willingness to be challenged on, and address, work-level details.